LOS ANGELES REVIEW OF BOOKS

NO. 24 QUARTERLY JOURNAL: WEATHER

EDITOR-IN-CHIEF: TOM LUTZ

EXECUTIVE EDITOR: BORIS DRALYUK

MANAGING EDITOR: MEDAYA OCHER

CONTRIBUTING EDITORS: SARA DAVIS, SARAH LABRIE, ELIZABETH METZGER, ERIKA RECORDON, MELISSA SELEY, CALLIE SISKEL, IRENE YOON

ART DIRECTOR: PERWANA NAZIF

DESIGN DIRECTOR: LAUREN HEMMING

GRAPHIC DESIGNER: TOM COMITTA

ART CONTRIBUTORS: JOHN BALDESSARI, LAUREN BON, CLUI (CENTER FOR LAND USE INTERPRETATION), ALEXANDRE DORRIZ, LAND (LOS ANGELES NOMADIC DIVISION), LATEFA NOORZAI, HANIEH KHATIBI, SATOSHI KOJIMA, SABRINA RATTÉ, LEROY STEVENS, OSCAR TUAZON, MARIO YBARRA JR.

PRODUCTION AND COPY DESK CHIEF: CORD BROOKS

MANAGING DIRECTOR: JESSICA KUBINEC

AD SALES: BILL HARPER

COVER ART: SABRINA RATTÉ, *BIOME I*, 2017, BIOMES SERIES, VIDEO HD, COURTESY OF THE ARTIST

INTERNS & VOLUNTEERS: RAYNA BERGGREN, ANI BEZIRDZHYAN, SARAH BONDER, MITCHELL EVENSON, CHARLOTTE MARCIL, MOLLY MITTELBACH, NICK RUETH, ELLIOT SCHIFF

The Los Angeles Review of Books is a 501(c)(3) nonprofit organization. The *LARB Quarterly Journal* is published quarterly by the Los Angeles Review of Books, 6671 Sunset Blvd., Suite 1521, Los Angeles, CA 90028. Submissions for the *Journal* can be emailed to EDITORIAL@LAREVIEWOFBOOKS.ORG.

CONTENTS

NO. 24 QUARTERLY JOURNAL: WEATHE

NOTE FROM THE EDITOR

Dear Reader,

It used to be that talking about the weather was considered Not Interesting. Weather was the refuge of the unimaginative and the small talk-y, people who didn't know how to broach larger, scarier subjects. More recently however, it seems like weather is one of the only things actually worth talking about. It is suddenly, unmistakably, urgent.

This issue of the *LARB Quarterly Journal* is dedicated to Weather. Our changing climate is of course, part of the discussion, as is the larger social and economic atmosphere that surrounds us. Amy Leach writes about the ongoing catastrophe that is life on earth. Claire McEarhearn writes about her experience fleeing the California wildfires. Aisha Sabatini Sloan interviews climate scientists about their dreams – how does the subconscious deal with the apocalypse? Molly Prentiss's short story meanwhile considers motherhood and survival. Carolina de Robertis writes about how the sequoia woods irrevocably changed her. J.D. Daniels recalls a wintery, disastrous trip to the desert.

Weather is everyday, local, ordinary. It's also enormous, critical, political. We should all keep talking about it, until hopefully – and perhaps this is going too far – it is banal again, and deeply uninteresting.

Medaya
Editor, Quarterly Journal

CLEARCHANNEL
004283

opposite: John Baldessari, *Love and Work*, 2014, images courtesy of Jennifer Siu Riviera and LAND
above: Mario Ybarra Jr., *Barrio Aesthetics*, images courtesy of LAND

Satoshi Kojima, *Mort à crédit*, 2019, oil on canvas, 63 x 47 1/4 in., image copyright Satoshi Kojima, Courtesy of the artist, Bridget Donahue, New York, and TRAMPS, New York

THE CATASTROPHE

AMY LEACH

For a long time, for about a billion years, green and purple photosynthetic bacteria had the run of the planet. They floated in community mats, absorbing light and engaging in carbon fixation. The atmosphere was stable, the environment unchanging: that period of quiet stability is called the Boring Billion. Then there was a Great Oxygenation Event, which ushered in the next era, called the Interesting Billions. Squeaky species appeared, and quacky species and screechy species and one very speechy species. Hadrosaurs appeared and crashed around, monkeys appeared and fell out of trees, snakes appeared and freaked everybody out. Wolves appeared and turned into poodles, wolverines appeared and devoured their betters, Betsy the fiddler appeared and played "Go to the Devil and Shake Yourself". Now, it is hard to know much about bacterial cogitation, bacteria being so sphinxlike, but maybe every once in a while they think wistfully back to that earlier era, before all the hullabaloo. Maybe they wrinkle their noses at us from their sludge lagoons.

But of course, if they don't like the commotion, then they should never have produced all that oxygen — for that is what they were doing, during the Boring Billion. Isn't that the way it goes? There you've been, meditating tranquilly, attaining such absorbing focus on your inhales and exhales that you have no idea how many eons have passed — only to look up one day and see that your respiration has been quickening hippos and hippies and tropical boubous, people singing "El Loco Cha Cha Cha," wallabies going boing-boing-boing. The Great Oxygenation Event is also known as the Oxygen Catastrophe.

And ever since the advent of oxygen, nature has been on one long upward march to imperfection — except for the popes, of course, who have been marching in the opposite direction. Over the centuries, the popes experienced something called "creeping infallibility," but for the rest of us it has been a story of creeping fallibility. The unicellular organisms just do not seem to make as many mistakes as us multicellular individuals. The more innards, the more errors, which is even true for plants. A vascular plant might mistake a warm winter's day for spring and send the sap flowing prematurely, but liverworts would never do that. To err is ash, to err is maple, to err is celery. Panegyrics are passé. Humans do not have the corner on fallibility, though we might have the corner on run-on sentences.

To err is manatee. A manatee might mistake a swimmer's long hair for shoal grass and start munching away, oblivious to the attached figure. To err is baby elephant, tripping over her trunk. To err is egg-eater and moonrat and turnstone and spaghetti eel, and whales, who eat sweatpants. Even the dinky species mess up, like the gerbil father eating his own babies like little ice-cream cones. To err is Pomeranian: the foster puppy I fell for turned out to have faulty wiring, to be a fluffball of fury, protecting me from all the nice neighbors, especially the nice neighbor lady in the hot red shoes. Sometimes he mistakes *me* for a nice neighbor and savages my ankles. Perhaps he was born into the hollow of a tree and then the tree was struck by lightning. Perhaps, just as he was trotting by the open door of a storefront church one summer evening, they were performing an exorcism. Now he is my dread fluffy little master.

To err is human: witness all the piano crimes, clarinet crimes, and drum crimes being committed on stages all over the world. Witness our inventions: to err is airplane. Witness our conventions, which seem to be standardized mistakes. Witness the mistakes where we get the early-morning sorries, and the mistakes where we get no more mornings. Witness our conscious mistakes, unconscious mistakes; fresh mistakes, stale mistakes; our wild mistakes and our timid mistakes, where timidity is itself the main mistake. Timidity turns you into a personless person, and a personless person is the same as a mooseless moose or a squidless squid. Oleg minus a leg equals Oleg; but Oleg minus Oleg equals zero. Stop phantoming around before your time.

To err is human, ye — however, as humans like to identify as all kinds of different things, grammarians, head honchos, paddleboarders, saints, etc., the adage can be made more specific. To err is grammarian, to err is saint — Saint Augustine sure had some erroneous ideas there. To err is

penny-pincher, to err is pagan: there seem to be as many different kinds of mistakes as there are identities — even angel mistakes — because remember that one time when you had to fire your angel?

Those who identify as sea slugs make mistakes, too. To err is sea slug; however, to learn from your errors is also sea slug. If you attack a Flabellina and it stings you, you can undulate away and remember, the next time you see a Flabellina, that Flabellinas are the nastiest, most maleficent little poisony pink-and-purple fringes, and you can prudently not attack it. From sea slugs we can learn to learn from our mistakes. (From Flabellinas we can learn to sting our attackers.) Once my borscht tasted strange, almost soapy, and then a pale green wax congealed on the surface, and a wick floated up, and thence I learned not to balance sandalwood candles on the ledge by the stove. One night I forgot to put the lid on the honey jar and the next morning I found a mouse swimming in the honey, in slow motion. Once I invited Gwendolyn and Gwendolyn to the birthday party but forgot to invite Gwendolyn. These and millions of other blunders have taught me millions of things. The Earth is no longer a good lounge but it is a good school.

Of course we haven't learned from all our mistakes yet. It was probably a mistake to throw all those sweatpants in the ocean; a mistake to give our hearts to telephones, televangelists, etc.; to celebrate the celebrities to that extent, while turning the baby cows into schnitzel; to let our herds overgraze the grasslands, rendering the land so dry the only water is tears. It was probably a mistake to get into such a torrid affair with Dogma, leaving Laughter and Philosophy to huddle together in the closet like two neglected children.

But after our substance thickens, our mistakes thicken too and it gets harder to outrun them. And sooner or later the undertakers start to gather. And after they are through with us perhaps we will go to heaven, probably bonking into the stars on the way. Or maybe there will be Billions with no modifiers, during which we will bonk into nothing, during which we will make no mistakes, which to some of us sounds slightly thrilling — those of us who feel like everything we ever did was a mistake. We'd stop making incompetent mistakes only to start making competent mistakes. Sins against decorum felt like terrible mistakes in the short term, but in the long term decorum seemed to be the fundamental blight. We'd even mess up on the paltriest projects — once when I was constructing a hovel I installed the wrong plank in the wrong place, which pulled the whole thing out of whack. Now that hovel stands there on the hill, a discredit to me.

If we could retract all the discreditable hovels, all the sweatpants from the ocean, all the soggy words, fishy words we'd said, all the musical crimes, all the imperfect pets; if all the mistakes were retractable and had hinges and would fold up and recede, I suppose we would have to fold up and disappear too, for even if we were not ourselves mistakes, some baby or other in our lineage surely was. The fallible wallabies would have to go, along with all the other furbrains. Goodbye, wallabies, goodbye catastrophe. Absent thee and absent me, the world would return to serenity, to the longueurs of perfection, and there would just be the bacteria and the popes left. Really the only problem with rectracting everything imperfect would be the goodbyes. For there has never been a perfect goodbye, not one, and goodbyes can prove impossible to retract.

REMEMBER

JASON PORTER

I remember winters. They were the most magical time of all. Snow cascaded down and to the sides, for months on end. You could swim in it. It was cold, but people of that era had ways of packing it around their bodies, helping them float through it without freezing. The literature which remains from those times is not entirely in agreement, on the subject of its prevalence, where it occurred, and how we managed to ride on it. Some say it grew out of plants. Others that it was manufactured in clouds that are no longer possible in today's temperatures. The animals of the time, much like the traveling snow puffs, and glacial outcroppings, were also magnificent. One, called an owl, was twenty feet tall with salted wings. It would swoop down and eat the polar snakes which looked like very small monorails. The reflections were of course dangerous, the sun, even then, a force of pain and torment, ricocheting off the scoops and mounds, the frosted hills, the buried trees. We all loved it. Because it allowed us a vacation from the swelter. And there was less disease. The children were called out of the mines. The sisters were allowed to bake pies in warm interiors while boys performed initiation rites that decided who gets to own what. And we all watched the winter sports. Ice gallop, snow jousting, sled ball, and elk rodeo. But don't listen to me. Set your virtual headset to 49a. See for yourself.

LeRoyStevens, *Floating World*, 2012–2018, umbrellas, metal stands, microphones, speakers, computer, electronics, cardboard, lenses, mirror, photographs, magazines, concrete, plungers, paper masks, packing tape, acrylic.

THE ORNITHOLOGIST'S HUSBAND DREAMS OF ANNIHILATION

AISHA SABATINI SLOAN

If I try to conjure what a biostation looks like in my imagination, I see a hexagonal white building, not unlike a yurt, but much larger, industrial, with hard surfaces and edges. This may be because I lived for many years in Arizona, where the strange beauty of Biosphere 2 looms like a museum or a spaceship in a desert city called "Oracle." Or I think of the glass-enclosed terrarium on the show *The OA*, where several survivors of near-death experiences are held captive by a scientist. A river moves underneath their transparent cages. On *The OA*, we are meant to wonder what it would mean if one of these captured subjects were an angel, but the suggestion is slight, more of a metaphor than a plot device, a way of asking what the word angel might mean outside of a religious context. I've long conflated angels with dreams because of the film *Wings of Desire*, where angels hover above the living and listen to what people are thinking. The angels become a way of outwardly describing the subconscious: since they can hear everyone's thoughts, those individual streams of thought become a river.

¤

I recently spent 10 days at the University of Michigan's Biostation, located on the south shore of Douglas Lake in Cheboygan County, Michigan. Ethnobotanists and climate scientists conduct research and teach courses there. I was invited to teach a writing workshop for a new interdisciplinary humanities program called Great Lakes Arts, Cultures, and Environments (GLACE), which offers students the opportunity to take courses in indigenous language and history, mapping, as well as creative, critical, and grant writing, all while living in the forest.

Here is what a biostation actually looks like: a road lined with uniform cabins punctuated on either side by pale green forest. The area was badly logged before the station was established, so the surrounding trees are relatively young. Some cabins are filled with strings of light and wood burning stoves and mosquito netting. There is a cafeteria, a library, and an awkward looking mallard nest high up in a tree above the volleyball court. There is a room that can be filled, for test-taking purposes, with bird specimens, which I discovered one day while I was lost, wan-

dering the property. The body of an owl caught my eye through a window.

Before I arrived, the students, who call themselves "Glaciers," spent two weeks studying with a poet and language professor named Margaret Ann Noodin. She and GLACE's spirited director, Ingrid Diran, have illuminated the history of the area for them — teaching them about the Burt Lake Band, people indigenous to this place, who were forced to leave when land near to the Biostation was set on fire in a purposeful eviction. In the 1980s and early '90s, the Biostation worked closely with local conservation groups like the Little Traverse Conservancy to acquire the location where the burnout occurred, including nearby Colonial Point, which includes a red oak forest. Thanks to this collective endeavor, the area is now protected land, known as the Chaboiganing Nature Preserve. There has been a concerted effort at the biostation to bring the history of the Burt Lake Burnout, as it's called, as well as indigenous perspectives on ecology and preservation, into the curricula taught in this space.

The students were transformed by their time with Noodin. They hold the teachings of their recently departed professor with a glowing reverence, joking about their new relationship to linear time. Their coursework was as somatic as it was cerebral, and it manifests most noticeably as kindness. They tell me stories passed down about the Band, about an old woman who walked away from the fire, only to collapse when she encountered help. They teach me how to speak phrases in Anishenaabemowin. We talk about how you might identify yourself in a greeting by describing the body of water closest to where you're from. The world around them is newly vivid, and they take pains to imagine the vantage points of mosquitoes and ferns.

One day in my cabin overlooking the lake, I get an email from a friend in Los Angeles quoting a book of poems she happens to be reading. The book is called *Weweni*, and it's by Noodin. I run to find the students to tell them. They are not so much surprised by the coincidence as they are emboldened by it, as if Noodin has sent them a wink. In "Woodland Liberty," Noodin writes, "When in the night I am weary and wondering / what the wild young Anishinaabeg of the cities will do, / I go into the woods and rest."

There is so much for our writing to hold. I want to cast a wide net around the experience they are having, or not net it at all, not to constrain it on the page. How can we let it continue to awe and bewilder us? We begin thinking about how to describe ourselves in this place through multiple modes. We make a graph that lists, on the vertical, things like: theory, allegory, interview, letter, vignette, portrait, photo, audio, field guide. On the horizontal: boat, intuition/experience, graffiti, dreams, water, cafeteria, language, homemaking, protected lands, bodies. We sign our initials at points of intersection. The students make plans to document the rising and setting of the sun, to make papier-mâché eyeballs that bring trees to life for a Michel Gondry–style film about dreams. They write letters from the perspective of fictional divorcés exploring the gap between rationality and intuition. They've sharpened their emotional intelligence while working with Noodin and seem eager to articulate something beyond what science can fathom. One of us weaves a being made out of leaves into the slots of a fence, as if to make a shape around one of the many absences that

"I couldn't believe Texas was real. ...the same **big wonderful thing** that oceans and the highest mountains are."

A HISTORY OF TEXAS
Stephen Harrigan

Big Wonderful Thing

A History of Texas

BY STEPHEN HARRIGAN

A tour de force by a *New York Times* best-selling author and master storyteller who captures the rich history of a state that sits at the center of the nation, yet defiantly stands apart.

Hardcover $35.00

Dakotah

The Return of the Future

BY CHARLES BOWDEN
FOREWORD BY TERRY TEMPEST WILLIAMS

In this fourth volume of his "Unnatural History of America" series, acclaimed journalist Charles Bowden interweaves his own biography with a vivid history of the American Great Plains to explore how identity is forged.

Hardcover $24.95

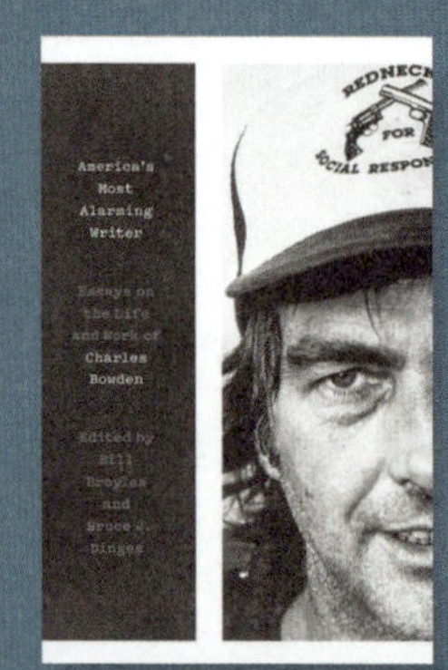

America's Most Alarming Writer

Essays on the Life and Work of Charles Bowden

EDITED BY BILL BROYLES AND BRUCE J. DINGES

A collection of fifty inspiring reflections on the life and work of award-winning writer Charles Bowden, with contributors who include his editors, collaborators, admiring writers—and a coda from Bowden himself.

Hardcover $29.95

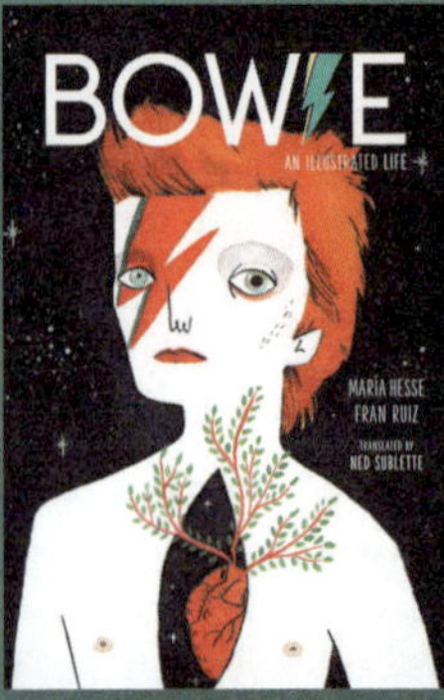

Bowie

An Illustrated Life

BY MARÍA HESSE AND FRAN RUIZ

An inventive biography of David Bowie, featuring María Hesse's comic illustrations of this otherworldly music legend.

Hardcover $21.95

UNIVERSITY OF TEXAS PRESS

utexaspress.com

Why Lhasa de Sela Matters

BY FRED GOODMAN

The first biography of the timeless bohemian world-music chanteuse who dazzled audiences around the globe and charted exhilarating new musical territory before her tragic death at thirty-seven.

Paperback $16.95

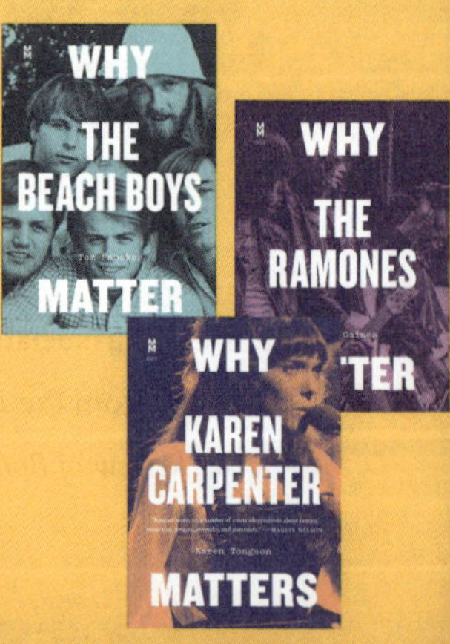

feels palpable here. We wonder how the scientists feel about all of our paint supplies and yarn.

¤

One night, I attend a talk on climate change. There is standing room only, so we sit on the floor in the hallway outside of the auditorium. The director giving the presentation says things like, "The world is getting warmer." He is starting off slow, just in case. Then, things get a bit technical. He makes CO2, O2, methane, nitrous oxide and nitrogen molecules wiggle in his PowerPoint slide. Then he says: "That's heat," and people laugh. The icons for molecules look, to me, like prescription drugs in the sky, or band-aids. He uses his own biography to contextualize the rise of CO2 over time: it has been increasing since he was in second grade. He tells the story of a man who went out to a mountain, opened a flask, and brought the air home with him. He quotes Henry Pollack: "Ice has no point of view. It does not vote. It just melts." I jot down phrases like: "We have 12 years to change it around." "Wet gets wet, dry gets drier." And, "We're looking at chaotic winters." Every difficult fact is dispensed in an even tone. He will say, periodically, "so," as if giving us some space to breathe.

What gets me is when he tells this one joke. The curve of CO2 on a graph is called the "hockey stick." He and his colleagues call the curve of CO2 and nitrous oxide "the hockey team." People laugh. It's a dad joke. But the instinct to continually bring the audience comfort — almost offhandedly — strikes me as generous, especially considering how powerful it might make a person feel to let despair just flatten the room. Before that, I had been focusing my attention on nervous tics. People shaking their legs, getting up to pee, fiddling with phones. We are all, without much outward manifestation of panic, absorbing facts of our unbecoming that the nervous system has no mechanism for dealing with. When the climate scientist makes this small joke, I crane to see his face.

I begin to wonder what the interior lives of the scientists are like, beyond their polite hellos. What does studying the apocalypse do to you? As part of the collaborative project I've embarked on with my students, I decide to collect audio recordings of scientists talking about their dreams.

¤

I speak with the climate scientist first. In his office, he tells me that he recently had a dream about flying in a plane across the Atlantic. All of a sudden, the nose of the plane began to rise, going straight up into a dark cloud. It curved, made a back loop, "like a loop-de-loop on these scary carnival rides." The pilot announced that he had lost control. It was time to make peace with the end. The climate scientist references this particular kind of dream as a recurring trope, "making peace with the end dreams." In a different style of dream, he solves problems (there's one about tree roots). What we end up talking about, mostly, is his concern about the social dimension of our coming catastrophes. How will we behave toward one another as things begin to change?

The resident biologist lives year-round at the Biostation with his wife, who studies birds. He wakes up every day and bikes to various weather stations to take down new data, noticing the way the plants have changed as the season warms or cools. But first, he goes to the yoga room in his house and does Pranayama, or breathwork. This practice manifests in his way of speaking, which is itself like a guided meditation, or a fin in the water, slowing even my breath down. "Lately my dreams have been pleasant, I would say. Mostly with friends. Although, I did have a dream recently involving a battle with a giant metal dragon thing, but I think this was inspired by a couple of things: the movie *Annihilation*." He describes the organism in the film, "the shimmer," which is both an entity and an area. He recalls a beer label that may have provided some of that dream imagery, too: "The bottle had this metal cobra robot thing with guns." He doesn't remember the dream well, but, "I remember waking up and feeling not afraid, feeling pretty confident, which surprised me."

The ethnobotanist dreams of walking. "Sometimes I dream about here, walking through these woods, or sometimes I dream about Guam, walking through those jungles." Guam is where he did his field work. "Just being in the plants, being in the forest, or being in the desert … almost like a vector, perceiving everything around me."

The outreach coordinator, who studied neuroscience and loves poetry, records her dreams in a journal. She reads some aloud. In one, she has been forced to recite an old Latvian proverb in order to avoid being turned in to the police. What wins her freedom is an actual saying: "Those without shame never go hungry." She has "Kubla Khan" memorized, a poem that came to Samuel Taylor Coleridge in a dream. I ask her to recite it, and my eyes flit to the window as she speaks. The poem feels like a wild iteration of where we are:

And mid these dancing rocks at
once and ever
It flung up momently the sacred
river.
Five miles meandering with a
mazy motion
Through wood and dale the
sacred river ran,
Then reached the caverns mea-
sureless to man.

A general ecologist works in lakes. She doesn't recall her dreams of late, but remembers that, as a child in Minnesota, she had a recurring nightmare in which her little brother drowned.

The associate director dreams of flying, which she used to do on helicopters during her field work in Alaska. "It's very much like the dream of flying, because … you're going slowly, so you can turn, you can swoop." Once, in the Arctic Wildlife Refuge, they "flew out to a stream, and the clouds came down." They could see that rough weather was coming. She and a colleague had to get out to lighten the helicopter and wait for several hours to be retrieved. "We had a radio, and before I could even see or hear the helicopter for some reason, I heard my radio come on and he said, 'Oh Kaaaaaarrrrrie.'" She manages to capture the pilot's deadpan, even evoking the crackle of the radio, in her impersonation of just two words. She laughs with infectious delight. "I'll never forget that."

A geographic information systems professor dreams, sometimes, about being caught up in a flood. He studies cities like the one where he grew up, fashioning models that demonstrate what would happen if that place were to be inundated by sudden water. He remembers, as a child in the Ivory Coast, that children were carried away by a current that swept down

streets and between buildings with little warning: "If you touch it, you are gone." In his work, he sometimes shows a video of a young boy caught up "in the middle of a very wide channel." He doesn't know if the boy lived or died. His dreams, like his models, afford him a kind of access to the perspective of that boy, and of the children he saw disappear.

If I were here to notice patterns, I might point out that a lot of these scientists solve problems in their sleep. I might also notice a recurring anxiety: how can they convey their research so people will listen? I might wonder if this anxiety about communication is an implicit acknowledgment that the sciences and the humanities urgently need to learn how to talk to one another.

¤

When I tell her that I've been asking scientists about their dreams, my wife sends me a photo of a page in a book she's reading, called *The Art of Mystery* by Maud Casey. This particular page contains a passage about Werner Herzog's film *The Cave of Forgotten Dreams*, wherein the filmmaker joins a group of scientists to the Chauvet caves in the South of France, which have the some of the best-preserved specimens of paleolithic cave paintings in the world. Very few people have been allowed permission to this place, but this film crew captures some of the earliest drawings created by humans. Herzog encourages one of the scientists to talk about his dream of waking up inside of the cave alongside the bones of saber-toothed tigers. Casey quotes Herzog: "'What constitutes humanness?' he asks a group of archeologists."

I go down a rabbit hole of Herzog's films, ending at *La Soufrière*, which was made in 1977. The film is about a volcano in Guadeloupe that is about to erupt. The filmmaker and his team of brazen companions travel to the island just as nearly everyone else has evacuated. They drive toward the caldera, encountering toxic haze. One of them leaves their glasses on the volcano. They are eager, for some reason, to enter into the precise heart of the catastrophe. On a helicopter ride, Herzog explains, "We got the impression that these were the last hours of this town, and the last pictures ever taken of it." The sea is full of dead snakes that have crawled out of the volcano. An instrumental version of "All by Myself" is playing as the filmmakers take sweeping shots of the evacuated island.

They track down three men who have refused to leave. One stands in the middle of an empty intersection, his arms akimbo, contemplating departure the way you might consider a trip to the grocery store. Another man is homeless, sleeping in a secluded area, cuddled close to a black-and-white cat. When they ask if he is afraid, he says, "Not one bit." He explains, "Death waits forever, it is eternal." He is wearing a dress shirt. He laces his shoes, which look like high-top, black Converse. His graying hair wafts in the wind, and he begins to sing.

As if to thwart the valor of this foolhardy gang of cameramen, the volcano never erupts. Like so many Herzog fans, I move between feeling charmed and feeling vaguely annoyed by the brotastic quality of this particular adventure. But after it ends, I begin to feel a bit of a chill. One phrase sticks out in particular. In that singular voice, Herzog says: "These were the last hours of this town."

LeRoy Stevens, *Floating World*, 2012-2018, umbrellas, metal stands, microphones, speakers, computer, electronics, cardboard, lenses, mirror, photographs, magazines, concrete, plungers, paper masks, packing tape, acrylic.

IN THE DEEP FREEZE

ELLIE ROBINS

It had become clear that he needed to be reborn, so here he was, on a rubber boat full of fools.

They were hugging the glacier, listening for the creak of calving ice, the Zodiac bobbing on the low waves. The guide was saying something about glacial retreat, about loss, about the end of something eternal and how senseless, how blind. He'd peg her at maybe 30 and not a real geographer; she seemed too young for that, too pretty, most likely window dressing brought in to sex up the science. Stuck-up, too: she'd met his attentions in the bar the first night with a series of tight smiles. His fellow travelers were hanging on her every word. Schmucks, the bunch of them, with their decades of desk life slung round their middles. The polar cruise, he had decided, was a Shackleton fulfillment fantasy for people who were scared of life.

Two years ago — a year, even — he'd have chartered his own ship, but with his celebrity soured and lawsuits looming, he'd had to tighten his belt. He'd spent long, late nights researching this trip, comparing routes through the Arctic at his kitchen counter in the Hollywood hills, in the quiet limbo after his residential treatment program and long after the invites had dried up. That, in fact, had been immediate: like a tap turning off the very day the first article appeared. *Star's pattern of sexual predation revealed*, read the headline, and life as he knew it ended.

Then 90 days of treatment in Montana, his blood boiling in the unseasonal 100-degree heat and the indignity of it all, relearning masculinity on goddamn horseback and acquiring a new vocabulary of apology that he would never, of course, get to use. It was far too much to ask that his version of events ever be heard, never mind that other men's crimes far eclipsed his, or that sex addiction was a bona fide goddamn disease and he'd done his time, hadn't he, shuffling off to the mountains to eat his humble pie.

The guide let the engine slack, and sound retreated, leaving just the ocean's breath. Hard to believe this gun-gray water didn't stretch forever; to believe it shared a planet with Los Angeles. The cold was just the ticket — he'd been right about that. How he'd longed for it in Montana: to be done boiling in his sins, to come slough them off in the ice. Certain scenes he was especially eager to lose. Shocked faces in an elevator, the weight of his dick in his hand. Red nails in his wrist. All that now freezing off like so many lesions in this pleasantly punishing pinch to the skin.

His arm squashed rhythmically under the weight of a large Canadian woman, seated to his left and encroaching with each wave. A different kind of woman than any he'd known, but what could he hope to have in common with civilians, after all this time? It was surprising, really, that none of them had recognized him, since not so long ago he couldn't walk a block without being made to sign something. He thought he'd seen a few flickers, back on day one, but if anyone had identified him they'd kept quiet, and all the better, really, since he'd come here to escape his own fame.

He'd read that life began in ice, or might have, chemicals animating in the deep freeze billions of years ago. Oh, he'd done his research, spent days with Frankenstein's monster, that poor, misunderstood creature, a product of his time, ousted by his time, now forever floating through the land of life and death. Jack London's dog, too, who came here and cast off the death-in-life of California. And the feminist writer whose books had swept TV, who'd filled pages of the *New Yorker* killing off a widower up here in the ice, picking him off for a past passion gone awry. He got it. There was no space left for the sexually assertive man, no matter that it was what women had always wanted. No need to tell him twice: he knew where the endangered species belonged.

The truth was, he'd felt dead for years, since long before those bitter old dates crawled out of the woodwork to kill him off. For as long as he could remember, he'd suffered the foggy lifelessness of having nowhere to aim, nothing left to conquer. He trained his eyes past the Patagonia outerwear, at the vastness: the eternal sea and the glacier, so bright, distant fire reflected on ice. He swallowed another lungful of frozen air. So strange to think that this had been here all along. A great

waiting blank that could never shut him out; where the goddamn *New York Times* didn't even exist.

He blinked against the glare, and the vision came to him full-formed: a drone shot of a lone man crossing the white wilderness. (He'd always been a visual thinker.) A hot bolt from his gut to his scalp as he recognized this first image of his new life. He'd hire a film crew and some local guides, and document his own rebirth. There'd be no soft stuff, no cruising. He'd go all the way to the pole — he was still in pretty good shape, after all; readiness for an action role was habit by now. His would be no cheap Hollywood reinvention: his icy rebirth would be straight from the pages of myth, a tale of endurance and renewal. Christ knew the world needed a new hero.

But now the world seemed to be splitting in two, somewhere distant. There was a rustle of expensive gear as all 14 of the Zodiac's passengers shifted. He followed the guide's outstretched arm to see powdered snow puff from the glacier's face, high up. The roar grew fuller and deeper, then for an endless moment, they all waited: the air, the water, the spectators. When the slab of building-big ice fell from the face, it seemed like a forcible rejection; a shove. The view from the Zodiac was dense with cameras now, and there rose a chatter of accents and cries as a second slew of ice plunged to the ocean. Over the racket, the guide was saying something about time, about the melting of millennia. *Metamorphosis*, he thought, and felt a swelling in his chest.

The action was soon over. The boat washed with navy Gore-Tex as his fellow travelers crouched to return cameras to packs, having captured what they'd come for. Cameraless, he sat bobbing alone, holding the boat for balance against the impact's swell. The glacier's new face was a deeper, fresher blue, and as he looked into it, he was surprised to feel a great grief welling from the heart of the last moment's exhilaration. To think that everything was changing all the time, and maybe without him. He gripped the boat tighter. His therapist had told him to expect sadness: there was no shame in emotion, she'd said, and he snorted, remembering this. As if he hadn't made a goddamn career out of his emotional acuity, while she was playing around at grad school.

The Zodiac began to pick up speed as it rounded the glacier and headed for the bay. The guide was saying something about summer sea ice, about scrambled weather systems the world over, about the end of food cultivation and the return of the dark ages, until the engine drowned her out and the Zodiac's nose lifted from the water. He was glad for the speed — he'd always been happiest in motion. The cold and the engine's roar and the world whipping by sent ripples through him until he found his way back to his relief, the vision of his salvation, his own life reanimating in the deep freeze.

They pulled into the bay, and the first balding guys began to dismount the Zodiac, each turning to help his wife. He was impatient to get going as the guide said something about shrub cover on what used to be miles of windswept tundra, about habitats and the great extinction. About soaking it in, just be back in an hour.

It wasn't exactly human, the force that pulled him up the hill. More like destiny: the same force that had propelled him to the dizzy heights of his life so far. Halfway up, he turned, to see the rest of them like ants, still crowding the bay, hanging on the guide.

He crested the rise and found a view of the ocean, mirror smooth. He'd been disappointed, he must say, by how ordinary much of the landscape looked: he'd been hoping for endless icebergs, but this view right here could be the Atlantic. He'd have to hire a good local team, to take him to the really frozen bits, and as he pictured these scenes his hopes soared again, a glorious unfurling after so many months spent stooped in punishment. He stood, breathed. Allowed himself this moment, after all his suffering.

By the time he turned back, the sun was gone, cloud-smothered, and he noted, too, the thicker dark of dusk gathering. He hadn't checked the time on setting off: he'd never put much stock in timetables — they were so restrictive, and nowhere more so than here. What was it the guide had said? Something about millions of years, about a timescale grander than any human could fathom, about hubris and short sight, and how small we'll find we are, how subject.

When he crested the hill again and saw no ants, no guide, he wasn't immediately worried. It was, after all, growing dark, and he'd been staring at ice all day. A trick of the eyes, no doubt. Nonetheless, he picked up his pace, his heart beginning to press at his throat as he drew closer to the bay, and nobody appeared, and the glacier crouched, and the earth turned once more from the sun to face the infinite.

Alexandre Dorriz, Early studio installation view and experimentations for *Economies of Small, or the Location of Capital*, silkworm cocoons exposed to YouTube search algorithm, "9/11 videos" played continually

JAMESTOWN 2019

CAMILLE DUNGY

Poem written on the imminent quadricentennial
of the White Lion's arrival at Point Comfort,
Virginia—which ship carried the first 20-some people
—mostly young—who would begin to build
this nation with their bodies—black—and blood

rock the other mother's babies down
slowly slowly slowly—maybe for four—yes
—for four hundred years —slowly slowly
—slowly rock the gone now babies down—
you know how a boat rocks on a calm

what rhymes with water rhymes with dry
your eyes—what rhymes with mothers
waiting at the corner—mothers waiting
at the coroner—these babies—their bodies
—they've kept them—hundreds of tears—

what rhymes with ocean rhymes with empty—
tell me—what rhymes with keep crying
I'll give you something—today too
someone's earth brown body baby discovered
who thought them no better than dirt

what rhymes with snatch a life and name it
building—this burden—don't end there—
what rhymes with help the mothers love
these babies—help them help them help them
—help them rock their stolen babies down

Hanieh Khatibi, *Earth Clay*, 2018, still video, color and sound, 5 minutes 18 seconds.

Artist's Statement: From action to intervention, this work responds to the crisis and unexpectedness of dealing with dilemma and duality while contemplating the circular relationship between the human condition and the earth.

BIVOUAC

TIMOTHY LIU

Whatever we were
about to start

stopped

when the loud
sound of rain

fell

on the skin
of the open tents

all around—

SOMETIMES SILENCE

TIMOTHY LIU

Sometimes silence feels like a cat
sitting on a warm amp, leaping

off for no good reason

only to land a downward-facing dog
before racing out of the room …

and sometimes I find myself looking

in a bathroom mirror and not seeing
anything I really like, wondering

how anyone could adore this face,

remembering how my students won't
think twice about sending a double text

if they haven't heard back in the interval

it takes three crows to cross a field,
not wanting to steep the hour in doubt

one moment longer, no!, why wait

for suffering to needlessly end
when love is just a heart emoji away …

and sometimes it's snowing, or about to snow,

and I can't decide if I should drive
or take the train, the roads by evening

turning to slush and I'll likely get stuck

on a turnpike glowing red in a sea
of bleary taillights as far as the eye can see …

map app on my phone saying

63 minutes for the next eight miles
and I don't know if I'll have enough gas —

Image courtesy of Chip Mandeville

THE FIRE FILES

CLAIRE MCEACHERN

It's 10:00 in the morning, and the air is almost too thick and dark with smoke to see the flashing yellow light on the emergency vehicle I'm following. I am driving my husband's truck at the helm of an unwieldy five-horse trailer down the Pacific Coast Highway, flaming tumbleweeds hitting the sides of the rig as if flung by a medieval siege. My 14-year-old daughter rides shotgun, her pet cockatiel's cage in her lap. The latter is whistling the sole tune in his repertoire: "Buffalo Girls Won't You Come out Tonight"; he sounds, per usual, like a small, feathered Jimmy Stewart. Behind us, the Irish wolfhound and her terrier sidekick are as excited as they would be for any other car ride, despite having to scramble for splay-pawed footing atop the jumble of hard drives and household objects that has reduced their cab space to 18 inches. The two cats, surely less amused, are crated in back with the horses. Our stallion, unaccustomed to female company, has spent the previous 40 minutes with an 18-inch erection, rendering him completely oblivious to the hundred-foot wall of flame steadily marching toward us. The following day will find me covered with bruises from the blows suffered in wrenching him off the three mares to which he had introduced himself, snapping through a stout lead rope on behalf of each. My own cheer is wholly feigned, on the principle that one shouldn't scare the children. I make sure to smile as we drive past the flaming entrance to the canyon road that branches off PCH to our home, and to which my husband had said he was returning when he left us an hour earlier at the coast-side equestrian park. I've never driven a horse trailer before. My husband had been loath to teach me given that, early on in our relationship, I had bent a previous truck's roof rack while pulling into the UCLA parking garage. Fortunately, the drive north up the coast to our destination — the sagging barns of the Ventura rodeo grounds — is mostly a straight line.

There is a long answer to how a New England–bred Shakespeare professor finds herself at the wheel of that truck, but the short one is the Malibu wildfire that had prompted us to move our animals to the public arena earlier that morning. This was not the first such evacuation. Living in the Santa Monica Mountains for the past 25 years, most of those married to a man whose family business has long been horses, I keep my car packed during fire season (i.e., year-round) with tedious-to-replace papers and the recommended three day's supply of clothes and framed family photos whose inclusion are less a matter of preservation, since they also exist in digital form, than a declaration of my preparedness. Our usual concern for these items has less to do with fires and more with car break-ins. My husband had spent the night monitoring the fire's progress online while I tried to rest; just after dawn, I heard his footsteps. They were heavy, the sign the fire must have crossed the 101 and that it was time to move the saddles and artwork into the yard. There they would have a greater chance of survival than if enclosed in the sustained heat of a burning house.

The footsteps were my cue to load the computers and small animals into my van, and roust my youngest daughter. Her sister was at school back east; one less to worry about, one less to help. When livestock needs relocating, hurried flight isn't the happiest choice; it is prudent to leave early, methodically and in daylight, even if it turns out to have been unnecessary. It always had been, in my experience — as unnecessary as the piles of flashlights and hoses and portable battery packs that the cowboy insists on stockpiling, and which always had me wondering whether there mightn't be a wee shade of survivalist in his hippie-libertarian streak. But part of my experience of fires was deferring to his. Such deference is not my wont, not just on feminist but control-freak grounds, but I have learned that in this circumstance a military chain of command is a relief. We have a fire drill: once the flames breach the freeway to the north, we trailer the horses, making as many trips as necessary, to local barns out of the fire's path. After the last load leaves, I take the smaller animals, the children, computers, and sentimental items — and, in recent years, my elderly mother-in-law — to some accommodating friend's place in Santa Monica or Westwood. Meanwhile my husband will unload, unhitch, and return to defend the house. The entire process takes a few hours. When the danger is past, usually the next day, we reverse the procedure.

This time, there were a few changes to the usual plan. My mother-in-law, who at 98 claimed residency in Malibu longer than any other current inhabitant, had settled into dementia in the last few months. Even prior to this turn she had been hard to persuade into the car during a fire, so two days before the flames leapt the freeway we drove her and a caregiver to a friend's house near Zuma Beach. Like most people around here, we calculated that the beach would be safe, or at any rate safer than the mountains; indeed, most people around here would spend the first 24 hours of this fire on that beach. The plan for the eight horses had also been tweaked: as the entire town was now under evacuation orders, there would be no local barn out of the fire's path, and no neighbor seeing to their shelter and care (the span of the Woolsey fire would ultimately reach 14 miles). We instead brought them to the municipal equestrian park, tying them at fencepost intervals in a sequence that kept pasture-mates close and — in theory — sexual opportunity to a minimum.

Setting up at the public arena with the livestock meant that I and the smaller creatures of our household could not escape to a friend's house. This was a first. My husband's shouted advice, as he left us to return to the house, was to re-tie the horses to the lee side of the trailer when the flames reached our position, and hang on: "It will be the worst 30 minutes of your life, but you should make it." (*Should?*) He indicated the direction from which the flames would arrive and that they would take 40 minutes to do so. Both of these predictions proved accurate. A Malibu native, with a family ranching history that extends back to the 19th century, he has been through three town-rubbling fires in his adult life alone, and can chart canyon corridors and burn rates from memory. For him, a fire is a drill. It has to be. Our home is a two-bedroom wooden kit house mail-ordered from Sears by his great-grandparents nearly one hundred years ago and built overlooking a winding canyon road that bears their name. While no insurance company will touch it, and no fire truck has ever visited it, it's lived through more fires than he has.

It would be 72 hours before I received word that both he and the house had made it through another one, with the customary aids of gravity-driven well water, burlap bags, a gas-powered pressure washer, and a weed clearance perimeter triple the legal requirement. Almost every other house on our road would be in cinders, along with 1,400 telephone poles, power and phone lines, fiber-optic cables, guardrails, well pumps, and all other modern infrastructure. The neighborhood had been returned to homestead conditions, minus most of the vegetation and wildlife. The 2,000-degree fire had removed everything above the surface of the earth — even, in some places below it, where burned-out craters marked the former root systems of oak trees. It would be over two weeks before my daughter, the animals, and I could return, and yet another before I could retrieve my mother-in-law from the nursing home to which the hospital (after the ambulance ride, after the sheriff's cruiser, after the friend's car) had transferred her once her beach refuge came under siege. When we parted with her she was able to walk, talk, feed herself, and sit up; after-

Image courtesy of the author

ward none of these applied. The insurance company nonetheless deemed her ineligible for further hospital care, dismissing a lack of electricity, running water, or access to the now-embargoed road at home as grounds for an appeal. Besides, I had apparently missed the 24-hour window to lodge one — that there was no cell service to do so was immaterial. My mother-in-law would die in her own bed three weeks later on Christmas Eve, leaving the eponymous road without its last living eponym.

So, as it turned out, our prudence wasn't enough to protect all of the lives in our care. Yet it feels important to establish that we are neither amateurs nor cavalier in our responses to the situation (or rather, cavalier is precisely what we are, in the etymological sense, of horse-concerned). One might even argue that the loss of even an extremely hard-to-kill old woman was coincidence, not causality. This is not to make the standard point that even the most scrupulous precautions are futile before the overwhelming force of the elements, nor the self-congratulatory one: that persons responsible for the care of domestic animals have a duty to possess the equipment and training to remove them from danger. Many people with horse trailers had no time to leave; some trailer-less animals were rescued through the daring of strangers who drove from hundreds of miles away. Other creatures burned in their barns; others yet were released from their pipe corrals in the hope they'd be able to outrun the fire. We lost less property than many of our friends but saving the house did not mean saving the outbuildings, tools, stalls, water pipes, pasture fences, rental income structures, or my sister-in-law's mobile home. Two horse trailers are certainly provident — we actually own three — but not particularly useful when you only have one driver. Nor did the mobile menagerie include my four hard-working hens, who burnt with their coop 30 feet from our house.

Judgment is almost irresistible in the wake of a such a disaster, even if apportioning it is a dicey business. Fire, like the floods that would follow it, belongs to an Old Testament order of resonant and retributive signs. It comes with an urge to retrace one's decisions, especially those forked choices where one's subconscious supersedes deliberation. Should we have driven north instead of south? Should we have packed differently? Why did I grab that object when I should have taken the other, far more useful one? (My husband says when there's a fire he gets to find out which of his shirts I like.) These re-treadings belong to the larger need to identify chains of cause and effect. As we are finding, extreme climate events provoke this sort of thinking; we now debate causality as a society, like a global-wide Frankfurt School. These causes can be small and large, precipitants or propitious conditions: stray cigarettes, untended power lines, multi-year drought, fossil-fueled economies. No matter their size, we will route such causes to human behavior — unless, of course, we are climate change atheists, or an insurance company, whose "acts of God" remain one of capitalism's last pieties. Such review helps prepare for the next time, we hope. But the reason we do it is because it comforts us, in the face of the incredible anonymity and enormity of nature's assaults, to feel as though their mechanisms can be identified and personified and compassed. It makes them seem avoidable. Or even punishable.

In the case of a Malibu fire, the latter hope takes the form of a distinctly *schadenfreudian* zeal, on the part of the punditry, to rebuke the hubris of those who believe they can choose to live in a notorious fire zone with impunity; build on the hillsides which will slide out from under their McMansions; who are willing to underestimate or even aggravate nature's ferocities in pursuit of her temperate beauties, and so on. The only information I received about my home or spouse in the days following the fire was the inference I tried not to draw from a television report concerning the house of our nearest neighbor, a celebrated transgender advocate. The report claimed, falsely, that she had been airlifted from the ridgeline as her house was consumed by the flames. In fact, she too had stayed to save her home before departing in her own car. This was typical of the kinds of details the media parlayed in pursuit of a moral, the story of crime and punishment in which human hubris meets Nature's slap-down.

Such stories obscure many things. For instance: The struggles of other, less privileged people who live here. Many of the homes that made it were humble ones, belonging to "old Malibu" mountain people like my hardscrabble in-laws, those who have partnered with this environment for generations, far more discomfited by the rising tidemark of urbanization than any fire. One neighbor — a lifeguard — dove into his water tank until the storm passed over, eventually emerging to battle the lingering spot fires that can really do you in. The refusal to leave one's home in a firestorm owes less to hill-hippie cussedness than to the fact that our homes were built decades prior to the invention of national park boundaries, building codes, or building permits that the city is unlikely to reissue, let alone issue *de novo*. Then there are the older empty-nesters without the years left to undertake a rebuild; or the many renting families in the middle-income tranche (yes, there is one) without a title to property to rebuild *on*, and for whom the new dearth of housing will likely mean relocating.

Of course, Anthropocenely speaking — hear how the term hints at the obscene — a family like ours and that of arriviste conspicuous consumers are indistinguishable. We are all carpetbaggers. Yet the moral of such stories seems to be that there are places, or there were times, more suitable to set up camp. (Here's a question: how long must one live in a place to be granted a forgivable claim to it?) Or maybe that it behooves people to settle in the future somewhere less vulnerable to "extreme climate events" — and where, exactly, might that be? Tell that to the developer-profiteers; they've already arrived.

Judgments also neglect the role of providence. While I had encountered the idea of providence in my scholarship, it was not a notion I felt terribly salient to my own life prior to November 9, 2018. But there are no atheists in a wildfire, if only because its vastness and apparent purpose testify to Something bigger and more determined than oneself: Super-Nature. Minutes after my husband left us to return to the house ("*Should*"?), county animal control officers drove up to the equestrian park — think dog catchers, except with stock trailers. At first, I waved away their offers of berths, on the grounds that I had been told to hang on so hang on I would. Some people led their horses to the arena while wearing flip-flops; I had brought water buckets, hoses, and a week's supply of hay pellets. I had two trailers to shelter behind. I was flattered that I had been thought capable to weather the storm, even in the subjunctive.

On the other hand, my daughter was the only child present, and she was increasingly aghast; the spectacle of her best friend's house being devoured by flames on the hill above us wasn't helping. So, as the last county van prepared to leave, some other part of my brain decided I didn't need to know whether I had what it took to gather her in my arms while a wall of flame passed over us. (Were we meant to stay outside the trailer? Hide in it? Would we cook? But what about smoke inhalation?) Offered a berth for the third time, I elbowed past the flip-flopped, squeezed three horses into the last two county slots, and loaded the five remaining in our own while my daughter transferred every household possession she could lift from my minivan to the truck. We became the last of the small convoy driving north, getting out with just yards to spare between us and an ocean of fire.

My husband later reported his own come-to-Jesus moment, when the three angled walls of flame racing toward him from three different directions — two more than he'd ever had to confront on previous occasions — met at his firebreak, and by dint of their respective forces beat each other back into an upright — and assailable — position. It seems you can fight fire with fire. As it turned out, our orders to stay would have been adequate, at least as far as our physical health was concerned (and one of the re-calibrations I found myself making in the coming months was that in our circumstances any other kind of health was excess baggage). When, some days later, he was able to return to the coast to search for us, my minivan sat unscathed in the parking lot, in it the vintage saddles considered too prized to scatter in the yard and which constituted his savings. My daughter had had no time or space or strength to shift them, and once in safety I began, ridiculously, to dread confessing we'd left them behind — that is, should he make it through the fire to question our triage. As it turned out, the only critique was that I'd forgotten to lock the car.

Nonetheless, the rodeo grounds would prove a far preferable place to wait out the weeks of mandatory evacuation to come. There we found individual stalls, exercise arenas, donated feed and bedding, courtesy vet and farrier care, and equipment: buckets, blankets, lead ropes, halters. For the people, there was wi-fi to soothe distant family and locate displaced friends, hot showers, and three meals a day delivered by Ventura restaurants and hospitals. There were similarly circumstanced neighbors and friends with which to compare scraps of news, and local volunteers who cleaned stalls and brought us blankets. I don't think I've ever been so happy to see anyone as a fellow family from the Malibu High girls' basketball team, who with their two goats, teenage daughter, and cool heads (they are both scientists) turned my lonely trailer into a base camp. Nearby at a strip mall we named "the corner of life" there was a Ralph's grocery, a Rite Aid, a Starbucks, and a coin laundry, where we took turns washing our respective three days' supplies of clothes. Coincidentally — providentially — all of our camping equipment had been stored in the horse trailer; I had sleeping bags, tents, cots, even a Coleman stove to lend out. There was also the hoard of battery packs, flashlights, hoses, power cords, power tools, and a pair of bolt cutters — I used them all — that earned me a reputation as the DIY Eagle Scout of the rodeo grounds. (When it comes time to survive, it is good to know a survivalist.) My husband, immured at the house by sheriff's blockades, would spend those weeks living on power bars and ramen noodles while trying to scrounge enough generators, gasoline, water, and pasture fencing for us to return when the roads reopened. I spent them in a daze which was part shock from the fire and part awe at the unknown goodness and bounty of others. Did I mention the Ventura fairgrounds are *right* on the beach?

Of course, in some cases what seemed like grace was, in fact, tax dollars. The uniformed figures in the barn headquarters were animal control officers — state employees, like me. The stalls, the arenas, the vet care — tax dollars. I have always been an earnest nanny-state Democrat — growing up in John Birch-era New Hampshire, we called that "overthrowing the government." But apart from the public schools, my sense of the benefits of government relies more on an intellectual ideal than anything I can point to. Discounting DMV frustration or the resentment of speed traps, I'd never really *felt* what government was. But it turns out that in a wild fire, government feels *really* good. It feels like a society with the imagination and empathy enough to anticipate that no one is beyond occasions of utter vulnerability. When my husband finally made it past the roadblocks to search out what had become of us, he suggested a banner for the barn office: "This is what socialism looks like. Love it or leave."

I would be remiss not to mention what small government philosophes may be pleased to hear — that what made the place tick were the waves of volunteers who came bearing dog food and clothing and toiletries and gift cards and *hours* of shoveling. It had almost been exactly a year since the Thomas fire in Ventura, and the locals are sadly well versed in what is needed. One garrulous woman whose truck bore the logo "Ventura Rat Rescue" (I'm still trying to figure that one out) saw my smaller dog shivering and returned the following day with two of her own dog's coats and a vat of homemade chili. Unlike the media, these people are still showing up months after the flames went through: work brigades of strapping surfers happy to dig fence post holes; a distant relative who drove out from Colorado with all of his tools, and instead of his annual far-flung humanitarian effort (last year, a Mexican orphanage; before that, well-digging in Nigeria) came to help us. My own good works, not unlike like my sense of government, have always been highly abstract and at an arm's length: the occasional donation and an unsubstantiated hope that teaching the humanities will make itself felt in a more attentive citizenry. These were strangers offering to do my laundry.

Life at the rodeo grounds was not all bread and roses. Our pop-up society bore many features of the more permanent kind, made palpable in an animal register. I was one of the few owners who slept on site, along with a few Spanish-speaking show grooms who, accustomed to life on the road, emerged from their trucks each morning in freshly pressed shirts and crisp jeans ready to commandeer the exercise arenas for their blanketed and show-clipped charges. At the other extreme of horseflesh was my sister-in-law's seven ancient and singed rescue beasts. They'd been found huddled together on the mountain the day after the fire and, rescued yet again, doubled the number in my care to 15. In between these poles were the strings of sturdy and sane lesson horses of riding schools and camps; the pampered

Image courtesy of the author

mounts of horse-mad little girls grown into women with disposable income, and a talented band of 18 hired out for film work, ranging from fuzzy mini-ponies to an appaloosa trained to rear on cue.

My own herd ran the gamut. There was the decrepit 35-year-old remnant of my mother-in-law's 80-year line of quarter horses, cared for like the ancient family retainer she was. There was also the glorious young chestnut mare my husband had bred and trained as a show jumper, and whom I thought of as "College Fund." Other heads looking over the stall doors belonged to burrows and mules, llamas and goats, chickens and sheep, ducks, roosters, and one cow — whole petting zoos and solo pets, the backyard creatures that amateur agrarians collect for the sake of servitude, sentiment, or scenery. (When I returned home, I found we'd become owners of three sheep. The neighbors had purchased them to supplement the ambiance of their Airbnb yurts, and abandoned them to the flames. We've named the ram Woolsey.) Some of these animals were much loved; some, like the haunted creature we dubbed "Mr. Goat" found alone on the side of a mountain, hadn't seen a vet or farrier or sufficient feed in years, and reacted to the appearance of each with terror.

Similar classifications sorted the people. Some of us were there from dawn to dusk; others showed up at noon, safely after their stalls had been mucked by volunteers; others we never saw — word was they'd decamped for Mammoth or Hawaii until the evacuation was lifted. Physically, there was a preponderance of what you might call palomino women of a certain age: some weathered cowgirls, broken-nailed and sun-creased; others were the human equivalent of their show-groomed charges. Some people shared the contents of their medical chests, and others swarmed the supplies like looters, including one woman I witnessed at 3:00 a.m. loading a full wheelbarrow's worth of donated horse blankets into her car. Then again, the morning after a flooding rain forced me to relocate four animals to dryer ground, one of the show grooms entered the stall I was stripping and wordlessly shoveled wet manure with me for an hour. One of the dewier, manicured types showed up one afternoon shepherding three truckloads of hay she had purchased for the group. Some of the noontime arrivals journeyed daily from barns as distant as Palm Springs. The battered car belonging to the horse-blanket thief was the only piece of property she had left.

There was probably no need for me to sleep in my horse trailer. For the first week, I sent my shaken daughter off to sleep at a nearby motel with friends; later, a borrowed travel trailer appeared and became a teenager bunkhouse. However, I still had the bird, the two dogs and two very unhappy cats extremely unimpressed by the two-story hotel I'd built them from the remaining cages at PetSmart. The thought of leaving them overnight was unbearable. In truth, separation anxiety extended to all of the animals on my watch. Some of them did require near-round-the-clock medical care; in a textbook example of how crisis can winnow the weak from the strong, College Fund had kicked Family Retainer square between the eyes, fracturing her skull and sinuses. (vet's diagnosis: "There's a whole lotta shit going on in there.") But it was more that tending them became a kind of sacrament of order. We all cared for the animals in a state of horrified apology for having made them prisoners of our own danger. Plus, nonstop chores helped to keep one's inner Hecuba in check.

In a natural disaster, the place in which one finds safety becomes extremely precious; when the time came to return home, I felt like I was being evacuated from the fairground. (Many months later, I miss it still.) For some, this meant motels that allowed dogs; for others, the Santa Barbara Ritz; for me, it was the makeshift mattress in the gooseneck peak of my horse trailer, and also the cozy golden peace of a nearby goat stall, where, warmed by the breath of Honey and Biscuit, a friend and I would meet for a bourbon nightcap. Absent creature comforts, there is nothing more comforting than a fellow creature.

It is a cliché to point out how easily we can be stripped, like hills of their vegetation, of the mental flesh that cushions us against the knowledge of our own animal existence, not only in its frailty but its ferocity. Upon our return home, we found that our house — a small oasis in a desert of ash — had become a magnet for surviving wildlife. Carcasses littered the hillsides, crisped in attitudes of flight and a still-resonant terror. The three Rs of a Malibu fire — rats, rabbits, and rattlesnakes — came in as close as the dogs would allow; red-tailed hawks circled overhead at dawn and dusk, while three owls took the night shift. One morning we found the body of a deer across the road, bearing the markings of a mountain lion kill: back mauled, throat mangled. These are not unusual features of where we live, but at that moment they were frightening visible. In this they resembled the surrounding terrain, its fierce crevasses and rock formations startlingly present without the mantling sagebrush — skull without skin. For all its seeming lack of life, this new place bespoke the ruthlessness required to count oneself among the living.

Such flaying can feel like a kind of time travel. When I told a friend and fellow scholar that I wasn't sure how to organize my account of this experience, she offered: "What it's like to live in the 16th century" (which would make the last several months a tax-deductible research trip). This suggestion got me thinking about how discussion of the economic or technological division in our country is often framed as a matter of space: the effects of globalization; the urban-rural divide, the top income tier and those below it. But surely these divisions have just as much to do with time. By this I don't mean *timing*, as in that phrase "left behind" — a phrase which suggests that the leaving was accidental and catching up possible (left behind like an umbrella, as opposed to on a sinking ship). I mean being shorn of one's carapace can make you realize we're all just five minutes from the 16th century, or, for all practical purposes — and in a natural disaster, the practical are your only purposes — any other century prior to our own.

My mother-in-law's plight brought this point home to us most clearly. It was one thing for my daughter and myself and the animals to return to the isolated fire camp that our home had become but repatriating the weakest member of our herd to these conditions was another matter. Caring for her in recent years had become grueling even with heat and light and running water. Now, because the house wasn't tethered to the power grid, all of these amenities came from generators and we only had enough gas to run them for a few hours a day. The hospice we'd been working with before the fire threatened to call Adult Protective Services were we to bring her home to these conditions. The insurance company suggested she check into a hotel; the social worker at the nursing home recommended a board-and-care facility in North Hollywood that, despite being far cheaper than any nearby, still wanted thousands of dollars we didn't have. We didn't yet know how badly she had deteriorated during our weeks apart, but we did know that given road closures, either of the latter options could mean never seeing her again. Strangers and proper shelter, or us and certain privation?

On the other hand, the same sheriff's blockade that kept us from leaving also meant that a social services agency might not make it up the canyon. She had been very explicit that she wanted to die at home (not so re: the funeral arrangements: "That's not my problem"). It also occurred to me that should the authorities exert themselves, I could argue that the legal standard of care was culturally — and in a way, temporally — discriminatory. That is, it reads civilized as modern. This was a woman who had lived in the Santa Monica Mountains before there were roads. She had ridden 17 miles of mountain trails to Oxnard High School on Sunday afternoons and back home again on Friday nights, falling asleep while her horse picked its way. (She was also California's first professional female jockey and Miss California Cowgirl of 1941.) Once, during an argument about gun control, she cited the danger of cattle rustlers. Whenever I proposed paving the driveway, she made tart comments about city people who moved to the country and wanted to bring the city with them. I brought her home.

It wasn't long before I began to question this decision: while carrying her from my car to the house, in the first rainstorm of winter, she vomited on us both. Her vaunted propensity to car sickness was the only part of her I could still recognize, and there was no sign whatsoever that she recognized me. I almost dropped her three times, and once indoors the only way to stop her trembling was to crawl under the covers with her, where we clung to each other for hours before the others returned from the purgatory of FEMA lines and built a fire. In the three weeks that remained to her we went through two years of firewood keeping the house warm, feeding the fireplace like a locomotive engine. When spoon-feeding her stopped working, we shifted to baby bottles, then to a turkey baster. She died as she'd been born, in a home sans heat, electric light or water from a faucet. But she was warm and kept close. Like newborns, it turns out, the dying need little else.

Living in the past also involves time in a different way: providing for yourself and for others consumes every waking minute. In a natural disaster, the only way to get most things done is to do them in person. Many systems and institutions, like insurance agencies and social workers, are immobilized or inaccessible or aren't designed to deviate from protocol. (And yet others are extraordinarily resilient. The morning after the fire I was stunned to receive my daily morning spam from Saks — *have they no shame*?) Going to a website isn't possible when there is no internet; calling the 800 number, which goes to a call center in North Carolina, doesn't help — a voice will simply inform you, after 20 minutes of checking with the manager, there's an "outage" in your area. People are the answer. You can buttonhole a lineman on the road three days running (bringing coffee helps, as does crying) until he calls his friend over in tech support and asks him to come fix your cable box no matter what the supervisor says. You can explain an elderly woman's plight to a series of doctors, who, if they are wily as well as kind, will determine what the insurance codes are for a totally fucked-up situation. Person-to-person care is essential to mitigating a disaster, and the most pressing incentive to do so.

Producing and perhaps preventing the disaster, on the other hand, is a matter of systems — climate systems, political and economic and social ones. Remedies, if they're out there, might be technological and must be structural, but their impetus – survival — is ancient. In the meantime, we shouldn't be too surprised if the earth takes matters into her own hands and forcibly reminds us of this fact.

It's now a year after the flames have gone through, and we remain without reliable phones or electricity. People have begun to react to this news with more wonder than sympathy, as if emergency might somehow resemble eccentricity. Wonder is easier than acknowledging that life in the new scorched-earth Malibu, so eerily like "old Malibu," might be what life in a lot of places is going to look like going forward. This fire is a mere chapter — perhaps just a few pages — in the story well underway. It may be the case that we've unleashed a juggernaut which cannot be stilled, only survived, and maybe not even that.

The earth will remain. After months of punishing rains, the plants on the mountains began to push their way up through the ash. For them, a fire is a very good thing. If there is any time left to us, we should figure out what needs burning.

Hanieh Khatibi, *"to whom the world is being related."*, 2017, digital print, 30 x 19.5 cm.

Artist's Statement: The artist dug a hole in the sand proportionate to the size of her body. She stayed in the hole, then filled it again with sand and got out. The action was captured in Carpinteria, California.

DAY MOON

EDGAR KUNZ

In the weeks after I left I waited
for someone a friend or her herself to walk

quickly up to me on the bus
or in the artisanal coffee shop and slap

my face spit on my hands call
me a bastard a real motherfucker by

weeks I mean the better part
of a year and by waited I mean I wanted

to be revealed by some visible sign
of my wretchedness a welt

to ride the ledge of my cheekbone
through the shit-spackled streets

of San Francisco a city ruined
by money and incomparably

beautiful it didn't come and it didn't
come and I grew desperate I stared

too long at strangers at Safeway I bought
boxes of clementines and ate them

like a possum on the train cramming
the rinds in the gap between the seat

and the wall I drank dark beer I made
no calls I sat on a hot metal bench

by a briny lake and tried
to imagine the lives of the joggers

passing in front of me their joys
their sicknesses and regrets it was

melodramatic I was useless I thought
of my friend who wrote a novel over

a long winter in Nova Scotia
read it once and buried it in the copse

of birches behind the house he chose
the spot he said for its plainness

so he couldn't remember later
and dig it up and in this way one

medicated season slid into the next
without incident gardenia bloom

persistent sun I fell in love
with the perfect voice of a Midwest

radio DJ from a station I streamed
on my phone called in one request

after another I fell in love with a video
of Stevie Nicks singing backstage

to her makeup artist sheer
cotton dress their harmonies breezy

and immaculate I woke around noon
to the thup-thup of helicopters went out

in my underwear and found a fine
black powder settling on the windowsills

dusting the parked cars a day moon
suspended in orange haze it turned out

a man who would go months without
getting caught was methodically burning

the half-built condo complexes one
by one one in ten thousand residents

is a billionaire the same article
told me though I could be forgiven

for thinking the headlands were on
fire again the intervals between

such disasters collapsing I caught
my neighbor's eye who was stretching

on her stoop in a fantastic powder-blue
tracksuit what a world I said and she didn't

seem to hear and jogged down the steps
and across the narrow street that stubborn

moon behind her rising or sinking
or neither it was hard to know

Mario Ybarra Jr., *Barrio Aesthetics*, images courtesy of LAND

SORRY I MADE YOU CRY

JANET SARBANES

My belly was bursting when I came from the gulf, and I looked for the driest place I could find to let my water go. You ran to greet me, waving your red caps, dancing herky-jerky in the dust. Some of you turned up your faces, crusty lips parted for my kiss. I made you cry, and you aren't the crying kind. Maybe that's what made me stay. Maybe it's what made the water keep coming, I don't know. I gave and I gave until I thought I had to be empty, I'm sure you thought so too. I'm sure you thought it as the dirty river swelled up and spilled out, flooding your barns and drowning your calves, taking your combines for a spin. I'm sure you thought it as the muddy water rose to your porches, to your neat little flower boxes. I wanted to stop, I swear I did, I couldn't see the lines between fields anymore, between farms, the lines that were roads, the lines that held power. I'd washed it all away, like a mindless scribble that didn't mean anything to anyone. Was it what you deserved or just what you got? I was coming down softly now but I still couldn't stop, not to let the light through, not to warm you where you stood knee deep in muck, keening for your crops. I no longer recognized myself, nor you, nor the place where we were, that great big basin of tears.

LAUREN BON AND METABOLIC STUDIO

TEXT BY PERWANA NAZIF

Lauren Bon is an artist whose practice, called Metabolic Studio, is based in Los Angeles. Bon and the Metabolic Studio create environmental art that is focused on sustainability, regeneration, and "self-diversifying" systems of exchange. Bon's examination of water usage is meant to catalyze political and social change, both in terms of behavior and modalities of thought.

Bon and Metabolic Studio are best known for the ongoing project *Bending the River Back Into the City,* which cleans the water from the LA River by diverting its path to the Studio's own onsite treatment facility. The water is then irrigated into state and city parks, as well as a larger distribution network. This project consists of a waterwheel, a cleaning facility, a tunnel that redirects — or, bends — the water, and the various bureaucratic needs (permits, forms etc.) for this kind of activity. The work is a performance piece, a sculpture, and an installation, bending into and out of traditional mediums. Ultimately however, it's a "transformation", as the Studio puts it, of "a water right into a water responsibility".

This ongoing project has its origins in a 2005 piece called *Not a Cornfield*, which was situated at a Los Angeles State Historic Park. *Cornfield* was a durational performance, which lasted for one agricultural cycle (from 2005 to 2006), producing an actual cornfield with the help of irrigation piping and planted seeds. In recognition of Yaangna, an ancestral Indigenous village that inhabited and moved along the LA River, the corn was "sourced from and returned to the Native American community", as Bon puts it. After the site was cleared, Bon created a new work with the remaining harvested plants. For *Anabolic Monument*, the corn was arranged in a circle into large-scale corn bales, which were eventually broken down into soil.

Bon and Metabolic studio consistently demonstrate a dedication to creating art that both sustains and returns. It's a return to fertile land, to a commons, to public space. In that return is a regenerative practice, both environmental and social.

Lauren Bon, *Anabolic Monument*, 2008. Aerial Views.

The *Anabolic Monument*, or "Cornhenge", consisted of a one acre large circle of decaying corn bales left over from the *Not A Cornfield* harvest. Lauren Bon was permitted by the Los Angeles State Historic Park to program activities within the boundaries of this work from 2006-2013, as the bales were disintegrating. Many events, rituals, ceremonies, and residencies occurred at the *Anabolic Monument* and over the years it became a place of healing and supported a biologically diverse network. Over time, the bales were broken down by the plants that took root inside of them and eventually the bales would break down to make soil.

Lauren Bon and the Metabolic Studio, *One Hundred Mules Walking the Los Angeles Aqueduct,* 2013. Aerial Views.

To commemorate the centenary of the opening of the Los Angeles Aqueduct, Lauren Bon and the Metabolic Studio surveyed the 240 miles of pipes, syphons, and channels that make up the LA aqueduct beginning in the Eastern Sierras down to the Cascades in Sylmar. This survey was done with a string of 100 mules honoring the labor force that was used to construct the original aqueduct. Photograph by Joshua White.

Lauren Bon, *Not A Cornfield (NAC)*, 2005-2006. Context Model.

Not A Cornfield transformed an abandoned rail yard in downtown Los Angeles into a thirty-two acre corn field for one agricultural cycle in 2005-2006. The work began nearly a decade of remediation of this iconic yet neglected site. This is the site of the last remaining undeveloped land of the native Tongva and Gabrieleno people, and the Zanja Madre or "mother ditch" that linked the LA River to the first Spanish settlement in Los Angeles.

Involving 90 miles of irrigation stripping, 1,500 truck- loads of clean soil, 30,000 pounds of corn seed, and 42 bails of corn fodder, the work signaled the beginning of a decade of experimentation in reconnecting land with water, engaging and collaborating with agencies and communities and challenging the existing system. When the year ended, a monument was formed utilizing 31 corn-fodder bales from *Not A Cornfield*, entitled the *Anabolic Monument*. This monument held the space for community and ritual activity, providing a focus for further civic and community engagement during the seven years that the bales remained on the land that became the Los Angeles State Historic Park.

CENTER FOR LAND USE INTERPRETATION (CLUI)

TEXT BY PERWANA NAZIF

In 2017, the Center for Land Use Interpretation (CLUI) in Los Angeles organized the exhibition *Desert Ramparts: Fortresses on the Fringe of Las Vegas*. This exhibit was held on Las Vegas's large-scale structures, used as drainage systems and as preventive flash flood measures. The photographs, texts, videos, and maps, all produced by CLUI, depict the intricacies of the flood control network and its extension into the farthest limits of the city.

The vast concrete channels of dams, dikes and basins, described by the Center as "massive marginal sculptures of aridity and stasis"— reminiscent of medieval fortresses — meet at the Las Vegas Wash, ultimately draining into Lake Mead. Miles of concrete and rock, the impressive network appears abandoned and dystopic in photographs despite its purpose as a safeguard, protecting the city from precisely this kind of apocalyptic end. The structures are a man-made effort to control weather and navigate water flow, and they aptly convey this power in function and form. Largely unused and idle, the structures also mark a paranoia or an anticipation for what's to come, concurrently appearing both futuristic and dated.

Waiting for the rain, waiting for the flood — are these structures waiting to be activated by movement, becoming dynamic and kinetic forms of sculpture? Yes and no. Land art and not. The infrastructure project can ultimately be described as land usage, and misusage — a meditation on place and presence.

opposite top: Anne Road Detention Dam, one of the flood control structures along the periphery of Las Vegas. Center for Land Use Interpretation photo from the CLUI exhibition *Desert Ramparts: Defending Las Vegas from the Flood*, 2017:
opposite bottom: F1 Debris Basin, Las Vegas, Nevada. Center for Land Use Interpretation photo from the CLUI exhibition *Desert Ramparts: Defending Las Vegas from the Flood*, 2017. Center for Land Use Interpretation photo.

THE MORAL CONSEQUENCES OF CLIMATE CHANGE

ROGER S. GOTTLIEB

I.

Ancient daily Jewish prayers changed twice a year, asking for rain in winter and "dew" in summer. Greek mariners invoked Poseidon to avoid punishing storms. In pre-Hindu South India, the goddess Mariamman was connected to both rain and healing. We have always worried about the weather — but now our fear is different. We don't just fear whatever the day has in store, but what the weather means. A snowstorm could portend something other than dangerous roads or school closures. We wonder: is this "unusual" blizzard a sign of even bigger storms to come?

Weather and climate are, of course, not the same. The former is what happens today and tomorrow — our experience on a daily basis — while the latter is the average, over time, of all the days. What we experience in the immediate present is weather — this storm, that flood, brutal winds, heat induced wildfires. And as the climate shifts, daily weather becomes a frightening intimation of a destabilized, dangerous future.

We have already seen versions of this future: this past year two and a half million acres burned in Alaska; wildfires raged in Greenland and the Arctic. This spring's endless rainfall put hundreds of thousands of acres of Midwestern farmland under water for months, ruining crops for the year. Mississippi's beaches were closed for the July 4 weekend because of a toxic algae bloom, brought on by heat and runoff of agricultural chemicals. In Florida, a similar bloom lasted for months. Temperatures rose over 115 degrees Fahrenheit in France, over 120 degrees Fahrenheit in India. Throughout the world, cities of millions are already running out of water. Sea level rise makes urban flooding not a rare "disaster" but a common occurrence — one slated to double or triple in the United States in the coming years. In 2017 alone, weather disasters cost the United States over $300 billion.

The great ice sheets of Greenland melting; the permafrost softening and liberating its masses of global warming methane; island nations in the Pacific evacuating their populations —10 percent a year until no one is left to face the saltwater-ruined fields and villages. We've already seen the crisis destabilize Syria, provoke tens of millions of climate refugees who have reshaped European politics, and led the US Department of Defense (yes, the military) to state unequivocally that climate change–induced social and political upheaval is an enormous foreign policy concern.

What's coming next? As the winds increase, how many cell phone towers will remain standing? How many illnesses will move into temperate zones? If three or four big hurricanes go up the east coast of the United States, hitting Miami, Baltimore, New York, Boston, who will pay the recovery costs? How big can FEMA get? And what other parts of our society — education, health care, services for the aged or disabled — will shrink to make up the difference? Best-case scenarios see "only" 50 to a hundred million deaths from the crisis. "Best."

By now there are an awful lot of people who want us to change our ways. Perhaps we will. But emissions and the percent of CO2 in the atmosphere continue to rise. And 33 global banks have provided $1.9 trillion to fossil fuel companies since the adoption of the Paris Climate Accord at the end of 2015. The amount of financing has risen — risen! — in each of the past two years.

Still, there are reasons to hope: the idea of the Green New Deal would not have been raised by significant politicians even two years ago; some nations are trying to keep their Paris emissions commitments; solar power is drastically cheaper than it was; Imitation Meat involves far less CO2 and methane: and some key Republican advisors have morphed into environmental advocates. All of these remain possibilities — policies and transformations that are yet to be implemented.

In the meantime, how do we think about a crisis that is engulfing us all?

II.

At times, natural disasters — bad weather, earthquakes, floods — have been falsely

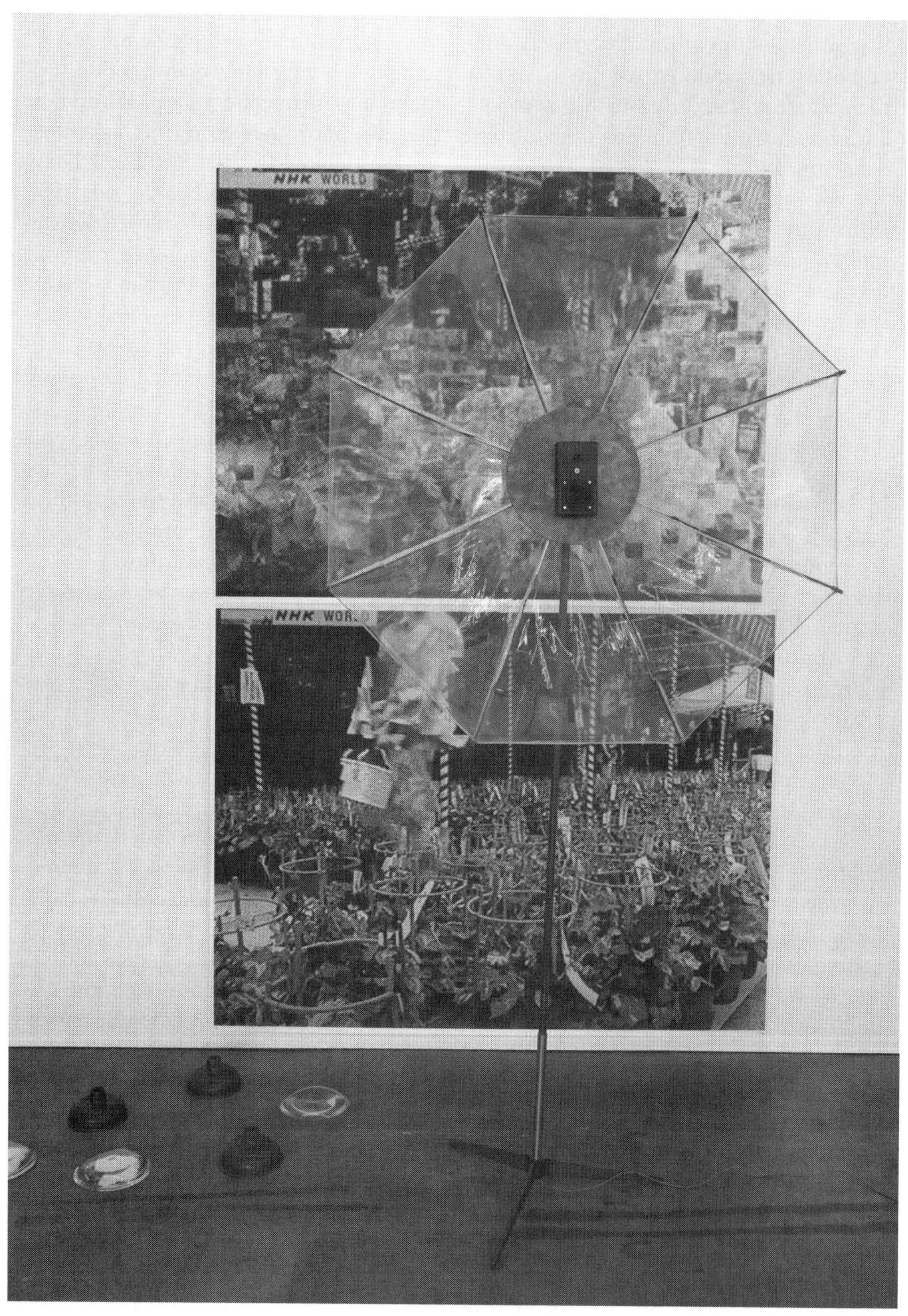

LeRoy Stevens, *Floating World*, 2012-2018, umbrellas, metal stands, microphones, speakers, computer, electronics, cardboard, lenses, mirror, photographs, magazines, concrete, plungers, paper masks, packing tape, acrylic.

blamed on people. Jews were thought to have caused the Black Plague; evangelical leaders have condemned gay liberation for certain catastrophes. But now weather actually does bear the stamp of human action. To say we live in the Anthropocene (human dominant) Age means that our species is now a global actor in ways it was not before. The weather is now partly what we have done.

Yet our species is not homogeneous. Different people have different amounts of power, wealth, and privilege. Therefore, while virtually all of us are morally implicated, there is a broad range of responsibility. Simply by living their lives a vast number of people contribute to the environmental crisis. But only a comparatively small number can make decisions that directly shape global realities.

Of the simply and truly guilty, what is their crime? Reckless endangerment? Profound intergenerational negligence? Manslaughter? Murder? Ecocide? We are not exactly sure, for neither language nor moral theory have caught up with the brave new apocalypse.

I believe that the clearest instance of direct and unadulterated guilt belongs to executives of fossil fuel companies who do everything in their power to bring more of their product into the world and influence both governments and the public to keep buying; to lobbyists for less fuel-efficient cars or fracking; to public relations firms whose climate denial is well funded; and to the politicians virtually employed by coal, oil, and natural gas. These people are not ignorant. As we've seen in the case of ExxonMobil, they know exactly what is going on and have for decades. And yet, they persist. The deaths of countless species and human communities are already on their heads, with many more to come.

Then there are political leaders afraid to speak the truth to their constituents, and who instead concentrate on supposed national interests, military advances, and ethnic or religious hatred. All those who promulgate what Greta Thunberg called a "fairy tale of eternal economic growth."

Cultural leaders — educators, intellectuals, theologians, journalists, citizen advocates — possess much less power than politicians, though they have also had an influence on how we understand our changing climate. For decades many have ignored the environmental crisis; or marginalized it into yet another academic niche; or advocated for other social justice issues while ignoring or downplaying the effects of the environmental crisis on oppressed groups. It is only very recently that the role of climate and pollution in racial, class, gender, and ethnic injustice has been widely recognized. Steeped in ignorance or denial, too many dismissed environmental concerns as "white" or "middle class" or a matter of privilege.

The vast majority of us are not, of course, executives, paid shills, or political leaders. And most people would just like to live their lives and be decent human beings. The owners of a local neighborhood gas station or the workers at an animal agriculture plant have no desire to hurt their neighbors. Neither do you or I when we drive to work or turn up the heat on a winter night. And yet, we are wreaking an ever-increasing havoc. Our participation in an unplanned and chaotic system, directed by just a few people, practically guarantees dire consequences. We have been thrown into — and are taking part in — a civilization destroying the conditions of its own existence.

The causes of the environmental crisis are complicated, far-reaching, and global.

Even so, I believe that each of us — including myself — must face our own measure of moral responsibility. This may be hard to take in, because the crisis is different than unjust wars, ethnic cleansing, suppressed voting rights, or a secret police torturing dissidents in basements. It is, as the mystic and activist Thomas Merton observed long ago, for the most part quiet, technologically sophisticated, legally sanctioned, and "normal." This is just how we live our lives: getting married and divorced, raising happy or unhappy children, advancing our careers or getting fired, caring for aging parents or facing our own diminished capacity, driving our cars, firing up our air conditioners, grilling steak, obeying the law.

As we do all these things, we suppose that things will continue as they have. The roads won't wash out in the storms, food will grow, pollinators like bees and bats won't disappear or replacements will be found. As we approach the cliff, we don't look toward the enormous drop in front of us, but backward, at how we've always lived.

When we stop and think, we know that every day we are getting closer to the precipice. That is why blistering heat or torrential downpours in some other part of the world can provoke an anxious foreboding. Yet most of us — certainly of the older generation — can't bear to think about it very much. From time to time we know, and then we forget. We keep playing along.

Why?

III.

The irrationality of modern-day human conduct is so enormous, so potentially destructive not just to the usual victims but to the caste of rulers as well, that additional accounts of motivation are needed.

We could turn to old social or political theories here, but they are not sufficient. The obvious financial benefits of disastrous environmental policies are only a partial explanation. While some of the powerful don't discriminate in their abuse or oppression, doling it out to strangers and kin alike, others will go to great lengths to ensure that their descendants enjoy social success and wealth. But climate change and other environmental catastrophes won't spare future generations, even if the one percent will probably be the last to feel the effects. What oppressor brings a bomb into his own living room, encouraging social policies that will guarantee a more difficult, dangerous, poorer world for his or her own children and grandchildren? And how do the rest of us, the 99 percent, live with the status quo?

Addiction might be a helpful paradigm here. Consider the mix of denial, avoidance, and inertia in addicts. In the grip of an often intractable and always physiologically and psychologically complicated disease, moral standards deteriorate, at times disappear. Addicts often know that they are destroying their own health, family life, career, and social standing, and that they are treating others despicably. But they see no way out. They are literally unable to think about the large-scale changes required by recovery: admitting helplessness, planning, extreme physical discomfort, psychological disorientation and the rest. Addiction does not leave enough psychic space to consider alternatives, rebuild moral and emotional energy, reach out for treatment, and contemplate life in recovery. And so the addiction continues.

LeRoy Stevens, *Floating World*, 2012–2018, umbrellas, metal stands, microphones, speakers, computer, electronics, cardboard, lenses, mirror, photographs, magazines, concrete, plungers, paper masks, packing tape, acrylic.

I am suggesting that it is not simply that we want what we want — the ease, comfort, and pleasures of our fossil fuel–based lifestyle — it is that we are addicted to these things. In our addiction we are frequently unable even to contemplate the basic shifts that are required. The notion that we might have to surrender something — driving as much as we want, foods from thousands of miles away, most of our meat eating, frequent flying, leaving all our gadgets plugged — is simply too frightening to contemplate. So, we deny or avoid the Bad News. If we have some awareness and acceptance, we still tend to downplay the full reality.

The long-term destruction comes closer, but not close enough to guarantee our attention. This is not 9/11 or Pearl Harbor. This is different. After all, it's just a lot of rain, or heat, or wind, or forest fires.

IV.

The great American philosopher W. V. O. Quine argued many years ago that beliefs are not connected to the world in a one-to-one fashion. Faced by experience that might seem to demand a shift in our beliefs — e.g., the reality of global climate crisis, and the way that crisis should take precedence over virtually all other concerns — we find that the experience is confronted not by a single belief but by a web of connected beliefs. Therefore, the new and potentially disruptive experience can be accommodated in a wide variety of ways. (In a remarkable and related example: The first researchers to notice thinning and an initial hole in the ozone layer over Antarctica didn't announce this potential disaster to the world. Rather, since they had no theory of how such a thing could happen, they believed their instruments were at fault.)

Thus in response to worsening weather, constant barrages of doom and gloom from scientists, and our own lurking fears we can manifest a variety of responses. The cruder forms of denialism are an option, but there are subtler ones as well: yes, this is awful but — and the power of the "but" is the distance between anything like the action truly needed and what's been manifest so far. But … it won't be that bad; someone else will handle it; I'm very upset about something else right now; we still have time left (echoing St. Augustine's famous "Lord, make me celibate, but not yet."); there's a techno-fix just around the corner; it's just too much to think about; my gated community will protect me while the poor bear the brunt; "What can I as an individual do?"

That it is enormously difficult to contemplate the most far-reaching and complex civilizational shift in human history should not surprise us, especially given the culture wide technological ADD we've inflicted on ourselves. Taking in complicated and emotionally challenging information, reflecting intelligently, sustaining tough conversations, making painful but necessary choices — how capable do we seem of doing these? The millions of people, particularly young ones, taking part in global demonstrations are a cause for hope, to be sure. But the hundreds of millions who don't participate are, conversely, further cause for despair.

V.

Is it hope we need to inspire us to action? Given the bleak realities of our time, it seems like the better question is not where we can find hope, but courage. Not hope of long-term success, but simply the idea that whatever the ultimate outcome, there is something that can be done here and now. We can guide our action not — or not just — on strategic calculation and confidence, but on a clear sense that whatever happens in the future there is a way to give love and promote life — of people, birds, fish, and all the rest — in the present. We can't tell about long-term success, or even survival, but we can try to support the life that exists today.

VI.

Consider trees. They put their energy into holding onto the soil, absorbing nutrients, growing tall, and taking in energy from the sun. In doing so, they support birds and insects and small mammals; people who enjoy their beauty, shade, nuts, and wood; and other trees, with whom they share nutrients through an underground network of root tendrils and fungi.

As the trees support both themselves and other forms of life, so can we. Facing dire predictions, digging out from storms, searching for increasingly hard-to-get water, picking up the broken glass from the "unusual" tornadoes and the broken lives from floods and droughts, we can ask, in a question both terribly simple and terribly hard: "What is the weather telling me? How should I live? Where can I give love to this miracle of life that has blessed us?" After we find the answer, we can act.

And, like the trees, leave it at that.

Latefa Noorzai, *Untitled (LN 169)*, 2018, Acrylic and ink on paper, 12x14 inches.

OUR CUSTODY

MATTHEW ZAPRUDER

This year was serious
in a dumb way,
and hilarious
like a grave cut
into a smile.
Dreams constantly
died without names.
We listened to the earth
say nothing, and knew
everything.
The earth a grave
we throw words into.
Seeds in a dark
arctic closet
wait for the new garden
tended by machines.
One whose name
will become dust said
in the shadow
under an umbrella
in our custody
only two died,
so it was a good year.
What can we say?
They were children
and will always be.

TUNNEL PARK

MATTHEW ZAPRUDER

eighty years ago
during those
famous dark times

when the government
paid men to build
bridges and dams

they carved this park
my son loves
out of a hill

the men needed
to keep working
to get paid

so they made
a long dangerous concrete
slide kids scream

down their parents
watching with
their hands

over their mouths
then dug
this unnecessary

cool aperture
full of obscure
shadows through

the hillside
to the garden
of famous roses

I don't care about
and finally some
secret stairs

no matter how many
times we have found
always seem

like they were
forever waiting
only for us

my son and I
went upward
his red shirt

kept disappearing
into the shadows
I became tired

from pointless worry
so we sat on
one stone step

and shared
some blue water
through the leaves

we could see
a giant crumbling
pastel house

it once was grand
its dark windows
still look down

on everything
it was so quiet
I could hear

the message
everyone knows
worse times

are coming
who isn't afraid
only the dead

we went further
the stairs never ended
we had to turn

back to our lives
knowing there is
mystery even

in the new world

Latefa Noorzai, *Untitled (LN 204)*, 2017, Acrylic and ink on paper, 9x12 inches.

LESSONS FROM A SEQUOIA GROVE

CAROLINA DE ROBERTIS

I.

Whenever I talk about sequoia trees, I feel the inadequacy of my words, how wildly they fall short. Some experiences run too deep for narration, though, as a writer, I continue to try. In the 13th century, the German nun and poet Mechthild of Magdeburg put it this way:

> Of all that God has shown me
> I can speak just the smallest word
> Not more than the honeybee
> Takes on his foot
> From an overspilling jar.

To speak of the trees, I could offer facts: sequoias live to be 3,000 years old; they can grow as tall as a 26-story building; they can reach the diameter of six people stretched out head-to-toe; their weight can exceed that of a hundred elephants; when wildfires demolish other trees, sequoias survive thanks to their thick and spongy bark. Or, I could tell you that the first time I entered the Giant Forest, at the age of 17, I experienced it as a sacred site, a temple to nature, a cathedral not only older than the stone cathedrals of the religion in which I was raised, but older than that religion itself. I was that bee. The jar overflowed. My foot was never the same.

I was traveling with my mother and sister. For many of us, 17 is an age when we discover what's possible inside and beyond ourselves. I was not prepared for the effect of the Giant Forest; though we only stayed an hour — nature is not my mother's cup of tea — it was enough to shift my consciousness toward, to use an old-fashioned term, the ecstatic. I opened my arms wide and leaned into a sequoia trunk. Alive. Prescient. All the history they'd lived through, the past two millennia, raced through me. Two thousand years and more. The tree stood calm, breathed oxygen toward me.

Who was I?

What was reality, if it contained this too?

What was my own tiny life, and what could I forge with it in the brief time I'd be alive?

I didn't understand myself yet as queer or gay, not with my conscious mind. I couldn't possibly have known that nine years later my parents would break off contact with me, when I married a woman, or that in the process, they'd say I could no longer be Uruguayan because I was gay, that gayness was so foreign to Uruguayanness, such a first-world invention, that it could expel you from the culture. In the late '90s, when immigrant and Latinx modes of queerness were not in reach at the tap of a hyperlink, my parents' words held psychic power. Their words would propel me on a search for the hidden queer narratives of Uruguay, and that search would ultimately give birth to novels, as well as to an authentic life once deemed impossible, with a family of my own creation that I love so fiercely it almost hurts, like staring at the sun. None of this future was visible to me as I stood in that forest at 17 years old, euphoric, high on trees. I knew only that the sequoia grove had opened me, filled me with awe, and shown me, if not myself, a vast, glowing complexity to which I hungered to belong.

II.

I returned to the sequoias 27 years later, with my wife, son, and daughter, wanting to share with them the sacred wonder I'd felt. It was the summer of 2019, my birthday week. On the first night, my six-year-old daughter threw her arms around a tree and said, "I love you, sequoia," and just like that I was accompanied in my once-private state of grace.

One afternoon, as we were sitting in a public plaza in the National Park where tourists from all over the world could study maps and nibble snacks, a white man in a red-white-and-blue USA T-shirt walked by us and muttered something about "environmental nuts and the gay Bay." I hadn't seen the man approach, and was slow to grasp what he had said. (Later, I'd learn that he'd been upset that

Fountain, Installation view at Visitor Welcome Center
Alexandre Dorriz, *Occident, galloping / Gilgamesh, swimming ; ML/OL 01-09 [Zoopraxiscope A (1/3)]*, (6) Xerox on Aluminum, Pomegranate (35°39'10.151" N 119°53'35.837), Conduit holder, Retail hanger, Binder Clip, Stainless Steel Cord. 2019. Courtesy of artist and Visitor Welcome Center.

Alexandre Dorriz, *Untitled Mirage 02-02 [First Study for Shah Qajar Chador 01: Occident and L'Orient (Zoopraxiscope B)]*, or an Exhibitionary Complex (The Lynda and Stewart Resnick Cultural Center No. 3), Cyanotype on Cotton Canvas (Inner Ring Exposure Time & Location 18:44/03.10.19;35.6539;-119.8927/CA-33 ; Outer Ring Exposure Time & Location 11:19/03.12.19;34.0638;-118.3595/), Pistachios (Iran), Exposed Silk (3 Silkworm Cocoons exposed to VHS tape of "Lawrence of Arabia : Tape 1" played continually for appx. 100 days), Cotton and Linen Rope, Pipe, Bolts. 2019. Courtesy of artist and Visitor Welcome Center.

Alexandre Dorriz, *Untitled Mirage 09 (Fountain)*, Eye Wash Station, Galvanized Steel Pipes, Donation Box, Pond Pump, Potable Water (Caltech Resnick Institute : 4,820 mL ; Los Angeles County Museum of Art, Resnick Pavilion : 4,789 mL ; Hammer Museum : 4,139 mL ; Resnick Center for Food Law and Policy at UCLA School of Law : 4,039 mL). 2018 work in situ, completed 2019. Courtesy of Visitor Welcome Center and photographer Ruben Diaz.

the park would not allow him to use a deep fat fryer at his campsite, angling for people to blame.) It probably didn't occur to him that members of those identities were sitting right in front of him: gay, environmentalists, from the Bay. As an interracial family with two mothers, we are often invisible in mainstream public spaces. But invisible and absent are two very different things.

My wife Pam responded immediately, and her voice rang clear. "I'm gay. And I'm right here. Please be respectful. We're all in this place together."

My daughter watched this exchange wide-eyed. This was her first experience with public homophobia. At six years old, she was accustomed to celebrating Gay Pride with all the pomp and joy and friends-come-on-over of a High Holy Day, a summer festivity more treasured than the Fourth of July. She adores her mothers and rainbow unicorns and rainbow flags. She's always been free to wear tutus and neckties, at times together, to live as expansively as she likes. You might even call her a child of the Gay Bay. To hear her home culture disparaged by a stranger was a surprise, an interruption of her world.

Meanwhile, the man kept walking toward the table where his partner and son sat waiting for him. He acted as though he hadn't heard, but what blossomed open in the air between us was danger. The plaza crackled. I braced myself for heat, conflict, anything, made a furious calculation of what I would and wouldn't do in front of my children. And then the strangest thing happened: his family rose from their seats and started floating away from the plaza, without exchanging a word, without looking at us, almost as if they'd turned into ghosts.

I took my daughter's hand as they walked past, and said, "There's no need for bigotry in a public space."

It was striking, how assiduously they pretended not to hear as they drifted away.

Over dinner that night, at a Park restaurant where the kids ate chicken strips and searched the adjacent meadow for wildlife through binoculars, my daughter asked to talk more about what had happened.

In the conversation that ensued, I told her I was proud of her Mama, not only for standing up for the dignity of our family, but for doing so without resorting to putting the other people down based on, say, the shape of their bodies, or the color of their skin, or even telling them off as jerks for what they'd said. And this was true, I thought as I spoke. When we travel outside metropolitan California, my wife is more of a target than I am. As a black woman, she is constantly disrespected in public spaces in ways I, a white-presenting Latina, am not. And yet, she'd managed to be gracious and declarative at the same time, stating an objective fact that hummed inside me now like a refrain: *we're all in this place together.*

Every time our kids learn a new layer of the bigotry that surrounds us, their world is subtly rearranged. The knowledge arrives in gradations. The public display of homophobia, sudden and flaring, was new — but they'd heard of it, knew of the concept. One of their sources for understanding homophobia is the story of my parents, whom they've never met. For years, I struggled with how to frame my parents to my children, afraid they'd be hurt by my parents' homophobia and racism. Over the years, I've been startled to find that, in fact, they're less hurt than baffled and outraged on my behalf. Why would we want to be around such mean people anyway? How could your mom and dad not love you the way you love us? Their world is so whole that hostile grandparents, far from causing a wound, become almost irrelevant, made obsolete by their own recusal, by their choice to float away like ghosts.

But let us be clear: not all aggressors float away. Just a few weeks after this family trip, a six-year-old child, Stephen Romero, was gunned down inside a bouncy house at the Gilroy Garlic Festival by a white supremacist seeking brown bodies to destroy. Bigotry flares, sharp and sudden. Gilroy is not so far from our home. My children love bouncy houses. They have brown bodies too. They might have been instant friends with Stephen Romero, jumping, laughing, doing silly flips, chatting in both English and Spanish, delighting in simple joys and in the very thing white terrorists cannot abide — the fact that we are all in this place together.

III.

Sequoias have a mystique of endurance, able to live so long they seem immortal to the human eye. But climate change is coming for us all. The recent drought in California did not leave them unscathed. The sequoias, these immense, seemingly indestructible giants, began to show signs of stress — brown leaves, dehydration — and a few have died, at least in part from the dry conditions. Even the largest living beings on this earth need us to protect them from what we've wrought.

The air is also affected. Pollutants have a way of sweeping right into the sequoia groves, which stand downwind of California's highways, cities, and industrial agriculture. Sequoia and Kings Canyon have the worst air quality of any national park. Packing for our family trip, I'd left my daughter's inhaler behind, thinking, erroneously, that air quality would be the least of our concerns in the middle of a forest. Her asthma is mild, and she hadn't needed the inhaler since the wildfires that had devastated Northern California the year before. And yet, on this trip, surrounded by gargantuan trees, my daughter at times struggled to breathe, for the weather is a mutable reality, shaping us all constantly, and shaped by the collective sum of our actions and inactions every day.

IV.

Lately, I've been thinking a great deal about the future of our climate, which should come as no surprise given the circumstances. But I've also been thinking about the phrase "cultural climate," how crucial it is to our understanding and survival. The climate crisis is not separate from our cultural crisis, which is also happening all around us all the time, a kind of weather system impacted by the rise in heat or storms or bigotry whipped up by the winds, caught in our lungs. Before the 2016 election, my daughter said of Trump, *We're not beautiful to him*. When I asked her where she'd heard this, she added, *Nobody told me this. It's just a feeling I had.* She was three years old.

Some people's lungs are more susceptible than others. Some of us live in more impacted ecosystems — people of color, immigrants, queers. The shifted cultural climate doles out harm unequally. But all of us are inside of it. It is up to each of us to decide how we respond to the weather around us, how we claim the commons,

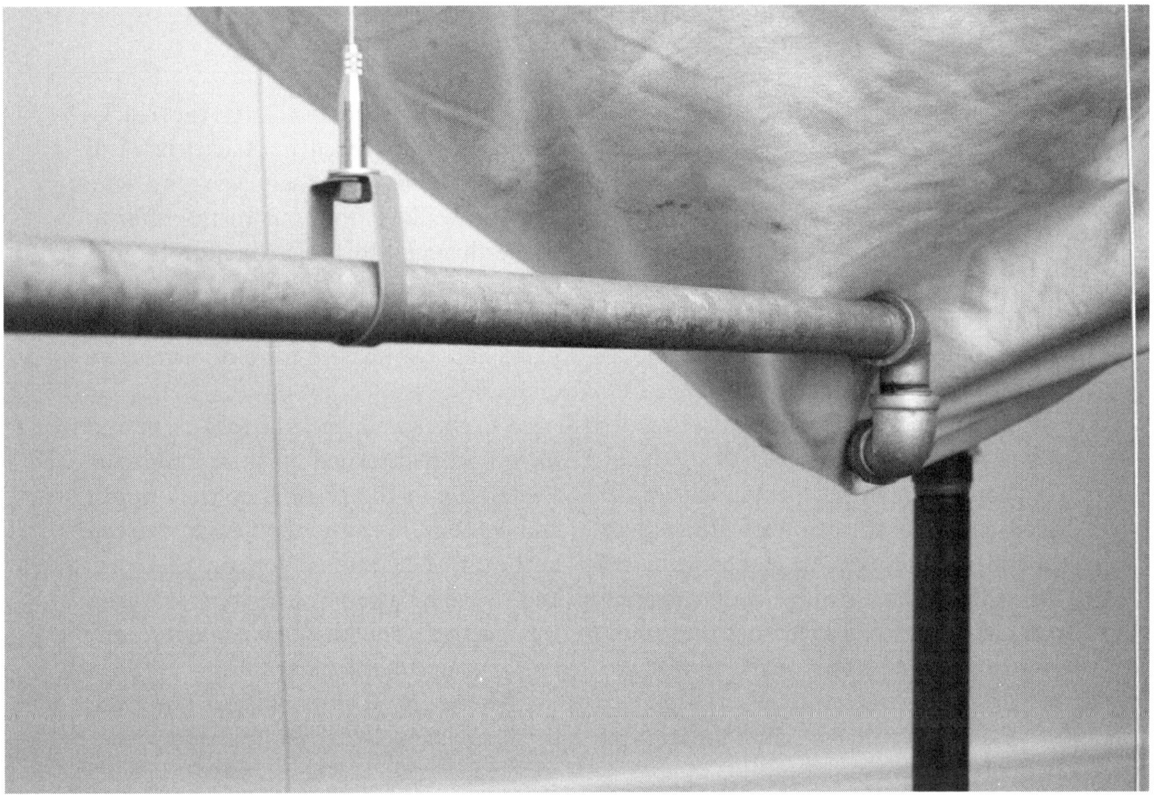

Fountain, Installation view at Visitor Welcome Center
Alexandre Dorriz, *Occident, galloping / Gilgamesh, swimming ; ML/OL 01-09 [Zoopraxiscope A (1/3)]*, (6) Xerox on Aluminum, Pomegranate (35°39'10.151" N 119°53'35.837), Conduit holder, Retail hanger, Binder Clip, Stainless Steel Cord. 2019. Courtesy of artist and Visitor Welcome Center.

Alexandre Dorriz, *Untitled Mirage 02-02 [First Study for Shah Qajar Chador 01: Occident and L'Orient (Zoopraxiscope B)], or an Exhibitionary Complex (The Lynda and Stewart Resnick Cultural Center No. 3)*, Cyanotype on Cotton Canvas (Inner Ring Exposure Time & Location 18:44/03.10.19;35.6539;-119.8927/CA-33 ; Outer Ring Exposure Time & Location 11:19/03.12.19;34.0638;-118.3595/), Pistachios (Iran), Exposed Silk (3 Silkworm Cocoons exposed to VHS tape of "Lawrence of Arabia : Tape 1" played continually for appx. 100 days), Cotton and Linen Rope, Pipe, Bolts. 2019. Courtesy of artist and Visitor Welcome Center.

Alexandre Dorriz, *Untitled Mirage 09 (Fountain)*, Eye Wash Station, Galvanized Steel Pipes, Donation Box, Pond Pump, Potable Water (Caltech Resnick Institute : 4,820 mL ; Los Angeles County Museum of Art, Resnick Pavilion : 4,789 mL ; Hammer Museum : 4,139 mL ; Resnick Center for Food Law and Policy at UCLA School of Law : 4,039 mL). 2018 work in situ, completed 2019. Courtesy of artist and Visitor Welcome Center.

how we shape what's next.

Not only that: our physical climate depends on our shifting the cultural weather we inhabit. We will not solve one crisis without also addressing the other. Anyone who thinks we can save the planet without dismantling bigotry may want to take a closer look at the facts.

The problems are inextricably linked, but so are the solutions.

So are the sources of our power.

V.

You might think the most mind-blowing thing about sequoias is their colossal height, or width, or incredible age.

To which I say: Hold up. Let me tell you about the roots.

Contrary to what people expect, sequoia roots do not run deep. There is no tap root anchoring these giants down into the earth. In fact, sequoia roots generally run a maximum of 14 feet into the ground — to anchor trees that soar 250 feet into the air.

Where do such roots find the strength to hold up giants?

They grow outward. They extend beneath the earth, occupying as much as an acre of terrain. And, because sequoias grow in close proximity with fellow sequoias, those roots interweave with the roots of other trees, forming an entwined, meshed webbing underground. It is this webbing, this interlocking community, that gives sequoias the power to weather fire, wind, centuries, millennia. Underground, they hold each other. They keep each other strong as they reach for the sun.

VI.

Everything you do will make a difference. I invite you to believe this. I extend my roots toward you, underground.

VII.

That night in Sequoia, after the chicken strips and binoculars and debrief of what happened on the plaza, my wife and son walked from our rustic cabin to the bathrooms to brush their teeth, and when they returned my son was breathless with excitement. An incredible thing had happened, a miracle, a form of retroactive divination.

On their walk back, he told us, he and his mama had turned off their flashlights to stare up at the stars. They were bright and copious, far more than could be seen in the city. He searched for constellations, and found a pattern in the stars. It was in the shape of a shield. What could it mean? He'd thought hard about this.

My son is 10 years old, and not given to superstition. His great passion is science. He dreams of becoming a biologist and working to protect endangered species, whose possible demise pains him to the depths of his soul. Once, when he was seven, he came home from summer camp and said, *Today a boy told me that God made me*. I explained that different faiths hold different beliefs about God, and that some religions teach that only their beliefs are valid and therefore apply automatically to everybody else. He thought about this for a long time, then finally said, *If God made me* — if God made me — *then God is nature, evolution, and time. Because that's what made me: nature, evolution, and time.*

It was therefore surprising to hear that my son had sought a message in the stars. But he was older now, and the Harry Potter books, which we'd been reading aloud together, had exposed him to the idea of divination. Perhaps more important: this was not just any night.

"I saw it," he went on. "The shield was for Mama! Because today she was the Defender of Gay."

His face was wide open, exuberant.

In his world, the stars could do this, could chime in on behalf of a Defender of Gay and shower her with cosmic light.

In his world, the stars were on our side, on all of our sides, prepared to back us up when we stand tall, tell truths, insist on love and justice.

And, if you ask me, it's his world that matters most, by which I mean the world of his generation — because they're the ones who will inherit what we've done, what we've failed to do, what we've forged or abandoned or risen to joyously defend.

THE ROAD TO CHOCOLATE PLANTATION

MALCOLM TARIQ

I

We leave Savannah in search of searching.
        My foot weighs down the road for an hour

until we cross over into Meridian — a journey
        I've taken before, not in this seat

but following my cousin's curious eye
        for history. At sixteen, I understood then

what I can't recall today. I remember
        the drive, the walk to the shore, and

the bus ride into Sapelo. I remember picking at
        a charred mullet fish fresh from the water,

roaming the heritage festival, scanning a Bible
        in Gullah — native and not. Today there is none

of that, only the deeper search of remembrance
        and belonging — capturing some stable place

between rippling gray water and shore.
        I drive further. In the back, my baby

brother's head bobs against the window —
        his first journey, already courting sleep.

II

At the port we board the school bus, its rickety
machinery — aged but useful — carries us

into the island, past Behavior Cemetery,
past the post office, past into another past.

The tour guide's heavy foot plunges further
and we lurch into the dense coastal Georgia bush —

the stick-like trunks tall and fallen, the spikey
growth of small palm trees waving us through.

Beneath us, the red earth brambles up
after yesterday's rain, the puddles bound

to form rivers that could swallow us
here on an island nearly lost to memory.

We trudge forward, and I see myself
in my brother sitting across from me

as if on a school field trip, unsure
of the destination but down for the ride.

III

At Chocolate Plantation
I heed a path trotted for me before.

I am this studious — furthering
and furthering and furthering. What else

is there but the tabby walls crushed
beneath my feet, nearly forgotten?

Like me, they too were shaped by the hands
of ancestors. Beyond, my brother

walks through and in the historical,
not privy to the storied. At ten years old,

he looks for the shells that have fallen
    from brick, those dislodged

or never having found place in stone.
    I wonder what he will take from this

and search for narrative, placing the hollow
    against my own for a voice, a whisper, a sigh.

We explore separately, seventeen years
    between us and what we believe to know

about heritage. In the end, we each take
    what we need to survive.

On an opposite shore, I ask what he has learned.
    "That the slaves made these," he says,

holding forth his collection of fragile fossil.
    He is the smarter one, having taken narrative

into his own hands before its forgetting —
    using more than his ear for the listening.

Alexandre Dorriz, *Occident, galloping / Gilgamesh, swimming ; ML/OL 01-09 (Zoopraxiscope A)*, 2019, Aluminum, Growlight, Unexposed Cyanotype on Mirror, Snake Shedding, Xerox on Aluminum, Pomegranate (35°39'10.151" N 119°53'35.837), Binder Clips

WALKING, LISTENING, ECHOING, REMEMBERING: IN THE RAIN WITH AND WITHOUT DAVID TOOP

GEOFF NICHOLSON

"Just walking in the rain
Getting soaking wet
Torturing my heart by trying to forget"

-"Just Walking in the Rain"
Johnny Bragg and Robert Riley, best known in the Johnny Rae version.

¤

One of the things I learned from *Flutter Echo* is that the musician David Toop is something of a walker. In fact, the title *Flutter Echo* comes indirectly from walking. He writes, "My first memory of a listening experience comes from a walk, a regular journey during my early childhood." He used to visit his grandparents in Enfield in North London. He describes it:

> Shortly before the railway bridge that took us over the tracks into my grandparents' road the path was bordered on both sides by a concrete wall. The narrowness of this path meant that the walls reflected echoes from our footsteps very rapidly, an effect described as flutter echo by acousticians. Like the fluttering of a moth's wings, sound bounces back and forth between the two parallel walls to create a "zing."

Online evidence suggests that a fair number of acousticians are in the business of curing flutter echo in buildings, but Toop would never do a thing like that. As far as I can tell, he doesn't want to shut down any sound whatsoever.

¤

David Toop is a lot of different things to a lot of different people. I would guess that he regards himself primarily as a musician, performer, and recording artist. He's an extraordinary multi-instrumentalist: on his album *Pink Noir* he credits himself with keyboard and drum programming, Telecaster, pedal steel guitar, false bridge and bowed steel, fuzz-wah flute, alto flute, gongs, genggong, sekai, mutator, Cubase, pelletdrums, Cherokee rattle, and Papua New Guinea flute. He was also producer. He's worked and played with some remarkable people: Brian Eno, Björk, John Zorn, Eugene Chadbourne, David Sylvian, even Timothy Leary. He was briefly a member of Flying Lizards, an off-the-wall pop group that had a hit with a "deconstructed" version of "Money." Much of his musicianship is decidedly scholarly, he's interested in how and why we listen, in the anthropology and shamanism of sound, sometimes pursued via expeditions and field recordings. It amounts to far, far more than the average interest in "world music."

But even that's only part of the story. Many people know him chiefly as a writer. For some years in the '70s he was involved with the magazine *Musics*, the complete run of which is collected and published in a facsimile edition, published by the Ecstatic Peace Library, who also publish *Flutter Echo*. Later he had a reputation as a mainstream journalist, writing mostly but not exclusively about music, which led to him becoming the author of books that include *The Rap Attack: African Jive to New York Hip Hop*, *Ocean of Sound: Aether Talk, Ambient Sound and Imaginary Worlds*, and *Haunted Weather: Music, Silence, and Memory*. As you see, he has a good way with a subtitle.

In these texts, he writes as though he's heard everything and has hardly a bad word to say about any of it, though he's most interested in non-mainstream music from the fringes. And yet, he is also the kind of person whose work raises suspicions about the usefulness of these very terms, "mainstream" and "fringe."

The writing goes along with being a curator and compiler of albums that relate to his writing. Some recordings share their titles with his books, and there's *Crooning on Venus*, *Sugar & Poison: Tru-Life Soul Ballads for Sentients, Cynics, Sex Machines & Sybarites*, and my personal favorite, *Guitars on Mars* (Link Wray, the Magic Band, King Sunny Adé, John Lee Hooker, Merzbow, among many).

¤

I remember, back in the '80s, I once had a few people round for dinner and I played, on vinyl, what I thought was an interesting and wide-ranging choice of music. I can't remember exactly what the playlist was, but given my tastes at the time there was probably some Adrian Belew, some Madonna, some James Brown, some Lee Scratch Perry, and I'm pretty sure I played Carl Orff's *Carmina Burana*. I resisted playing an album I had of recordings of diesel electric locomotives because I knew from experience that it was a room-clearer, but I do know that I played something by the Spontaneous Music Ensemble, a high-water mark in free jazz improvisation. David Toop was never a member though he played with many of the alumni. But at my dinner party, that was what did it. After a few minutes of the record, one of the guests said he'd had more than enough, and accused me of being a pretentious poseur, a popinjay, trying way too hard to be cool. All these years after the event, who's to say he was wrong? But it hadn't felt that way to me at the time, I was just trying to be a quirky and adventurous DJ. My guest stormed off into the night, and into the English rain.

¤

A word to the wise for the unwary and those unfamiliar with the English climate. If you listen to the Beatles' "I Am the Walrus," you'll hear the lines,

> Sitting in an English garden
> Waiting for the sun
> If the sun don't come you get a
> tan
> From standing in the English
> rain.

Kids, this is blatantly untrue. The English rain may do any number of things to you, but it will very definitely not provide you with a tan.

¤

I have never been invited to David Toop's for dinner, and I don't expect to be, but I imagine his playlist would make my own selections of music look like the tamest easy listening. Some of the chapters in *Flutter Echo* end with a list of the music he was listening to at various times in his life. One list headed "My Tastes in 1976–9" includes Dr. Alimantado, the Slits, Evelyn "Champagne" King, and *Oiseaux de Venezuela* — an album of actual bird song recorded by Jean C. Roché. Between 1998 and 2015, he was listening to Christian Fennesz, Ami Yoshida, and Haruomi Hosono. I think it's forgivable not to have heard of every one of the artists Toop appreciates, but the fact is that his, and my, eclecticism, doesn't mean so very much anymore. Today, eclecticism may not involve much more than having a Spotify playlist. As Simon Reynolds has said in an article in *The Wire*, "We're all David Toop Now." Reynolds frets, quite reasonably it seems to me, about whether the quest for "exotic" or "fringe" music "has anything like the same value when it's achieved effortlessly." And at times even Toop seems to be exhausted by it all. He writes at the start of *Haunted Weather* that "trying to listen to everything has almost destroyed my desire to listen to anything." But this was evidently a temporary state of affairs. His ears are currently open again for business.

The title *Haunted Weather* takes its inspiration partly from an entry he found in a diary belonging to his late father. The entry runs in full, "A slight breeze." Toop says he remembers it "if only for the lack of excitement." Toop's current position seems to be that the entire planet, the atmosphere, the ether, is not just haunted but drenched by sounds and signals, both "natural" and "manmade." He also writes about a Finnish duo Pan Sonic, whose music he says "can feel as physical as a weather system." Certainly most of us are familiar with the experience of being "blown away" by certain particularly intense live acts.

¤

Toop is an honest and straightforward storyteller, but there were times reading *Flutter Echo* when it seemed to me that he was looking at his life and work through the wrong end of a telescope. Some of the descriptions of his musical activities are perfunctory and opaque, like this one relating to his album *Buried Dreams*, made with Max Eastley:

> Music technology was beginning to allow more plasticity, a more sculptural approach in which time could be out of joint, tradition clashing with futurity, at the same time it was generating the kind of personalized listening and cross-genre cassette playlists that anticipated a future of digital downloads and MP3 players.

Well yes, possibly, but this sounds more like part of a grant application than a memoir.

Inevitably the personal life is inseparable from the musical life. Toop tells us that at one point in the early '70s he lived with the artist Marie Yates, and together they did "Field Workings," described by Toop as "walking and working from within the self and under the sky, deeply private even though conducted on open land and documented." She made environmental sculptures, he made recordings, one of which consisted of "hanging my microphone on a wire fence, then walking away as I played sounds that were snatched from me by the wind…"

This sounds a good deal less wearying than Toop's 30-year professional relationship with sound poet Bob Cobbing, who would "subvert" performances by getting drunk while a small group of musicians tried to "interpret" his work. Toop writes, "Then there was a nightmarish performance by the sextet at the Poetry Society on the 1970s, Bob effectively creating a band within a band as he felt the music moving away from the poems. Paul Burwell standing in front of us at one point and shouting 'Band!' in an attempt to restore unity." I find this hard to envisage very precisely, but it still sounds like more fun than many poetry readings I've been to.

Toop is obviously much more comfortable discussing live performances and the weather than talking about his emotional or personal state. The "intensity of being alive" appears easier to approach when it's rendered on a larger scale. The book founders when Toop reorients to painful episodes in his personal life. After the suicide of his wife, the mother of his daughter, he writes, "What followed was vivid chaotic and unbearable to recall." This may well be true but if you're writing a memoir, I think there's a certain duty to recall the unbearable. Instead he gets tangled up in a description of a Japanese film about suicide — *Maborosi* — and then he's off describing Australian Aboriginal bereavement rituals. You could say (à la Eno) that this is an oblique strategy, or you could say it's an avoidance technique.

I found myself thinking about the old T. S. Eliot chestnut that "poetry is not a turning loose of emotion, but an escape from emotion; it is not the expression of personality, but an escape from personality." I wonder if Toop would agree. And then, since the book inevitably leads into notions of memory and sound, I thought of the lines from "Burnt Norton,"

> Footfalls echo in the memory,
> down the passage we did not take,
> towards the door we never opened,
> into the rose garden. My words echo,
> Thus in your mind.

That old repeated echo again, and I was also remembering from the same poem, "The moment in the arbor where the rain beat." That idea of rain as a rhythm, as a beat, seems right on the money in this context.

¤

A song that completely misuses rain as a metaphor for amatory absence? Everything But The Girl's "Like Deserts Miss the Rain," with the line "And I miss you like deserts miss the rain." The fact is, deserts don't in any sense "miss" the rain. Even if we accept some version of the pathetic fallacy, deserts sit there quite stoically, unmoved whether the rain comes or not.

Song that most egregiously misunderstands what rain even is? Fleetwood Mac's "Dreams" and that line "Thunder only happens when it's raining." I mean really, it just doesn't. Thunder neither requires nor always accompanies rain, and vice versa. You know that, I know that, why the heck doesn't Stevie Nicks know it? David Toop does, I'm sure.

¤

Flutter Echo was first published in a Japanese translation by the Tokyo imprint Du Books: an unusual way into print by any publishing standard. This English-language edition is published by Ecstatic Peace Library, lovingly run by Eva Prinz and Thurston Moore, the latter of whom contributes a foreword.

To celebrate publication of the book and Toop's 70th birthday he had a three-day residency at Café Oto in London. The evening I went to was titled General Strike, the name of a group Toop was once part of, with David Cunningham and Steve Beresford. All three were there that night, along with some new blood, including Thurston Moore himself. (You may remember the song "In Silver Rain With a Paper Key" from his solo album *Demolished Thoughts*, or Sonic Youth's "Rain on Tin" from *Murray Street*.) Moore was seated for the gig, playing with intensity but noticeably not as loudly as Toop, and he seemed to be holding back, not necessarily in a bad way. I thought that he might want to crank things up to 11, create walls of feedback, and roll around the ground with his guitar, the way he's been known to. But this time he was very decorous, perhaps showing the deference due to an author from his publisher, which is rare indeed. One wag I spoke to in the audience said this should have been the house band for the *Twin Peaks* reboot.

¤

In the last chapter of *Exotica*, Toop describes a festival that took place in Gunnersbury Park in West London, featuring musicians and dancers from Papua New Guinea. He writes, "As the first dance for a Moka exchange ceremony began, the dancers dressed in Bird of Paradise feathers and long striped aprons, the rain fell. [...] The temperature plummeted, the sky darkened, the heavens opened."

Fortunately, there was a marquee nearby into which the performers ran.

> We huddled together like guests at a bizarre wedding reception: near naked women, their faces painted red, crushed against the Mud Men, their masks looking more like an inconvenience than an apparition. [...] Cigarettes were smoked. Tea was passed around in plastic cups. [...] For a passing second, nobody was exotic, though some of us were more suitably dressed for the environment than others.

The chapter is titled "Rain Dance."

¤

"And all over the world, strangers
Talk only about the weather."

-Tom Waits, "Strange Weather"

BEYOND JUST WHAT THE APPLE MEANT TO EVE

MICHELLE DOMINIQUE BURK

I can never love rain because of you.

A man was struck by lightning while drinking tea
at his kitchen table.

Another — accused of beating his wife —
decided to fly his plane
into his mother-in-law's living room
during a hurricane.

Winter forces its way into me
like your silhouette.

In this particular dark
I'm recounting my childhood,
when the cloud above my head
was white-glazed linen.

I'm thinking about how you've always saved
the best bruises for me — exactly the
ones I ask for, if not the ones I deserve.

I thought the word *no* was meant to be useful.

It's supposed to stand in
for exactly everything:
the cologne on the sweaty collar of a shirt,
multicolored hot springs,
miniature clay beings,
hands clamoring up my skirt.

I'm sure that I said it.

Every hailstorm chases me, every new city
is an old wound of you, reopening.

I'm thinking of black spatter against bark —
of God angrily striking a match
against what was once a sky and making electricity.

Afterward, there was light, or morning, maybe,
and you said you couldn't have heard me
over all the thunder.

No always gets lost in whatever surrounds it.

Maybe Eve didn't really want that apple
but was forced to eat it anyway.

Fountain, Installation view at Visitor Welcome Center

Alexandre Dorriz, *Occident, galloping / Gilgamesh, swimming ; ML/OL 01-09 [Zoopraxiscope A (1/3)]*, (6) Xerox on Aluminum, Pomegranate (35°39'10.151" N 119°53'35.837), Conduit holder, Retail hanger, Binder Clip, Stainless Steel Cord. 2019. Courtesy of artist and Visitor Welcome Center.

Alexandre Dorriz, *Untitled Mirage 02-02 [First Study for Shah Qajar Chador 01: Occident and L'Orient (Zoopraxiscope B)], or an Exhibitionary Complex (The Lynda and Stewart Resnick Cultural Center No. 3)*, Cyanotype on Cotton Canvas (Inner Ring Exposure Time & Location 18:44/03.10.19;35.6539;-119.8927/CA-33 ; Outer Ring Exposure Time & Location 11:19/03.12.19;34.0638;-118.3595/), Pistachios (Iran), Exposed Silk (3 Silkworm Cocoons exposed to VHS tape of "Lawrence of Arabia : Tape 1" played continually for appx. 100 days), Cotton and Linen Rope, Pipe, Bolts. 2019. Courtesy of artist and Visitor Welcome Center.

Alexandre Dorriz, *Untitled Mirage 09 (Fountain)*, Eye Wash Station, Galvanized Steel Pipes, Donation Box, Pond Pump, Potable Water (Caltech Resnick Institute : 4,820 mL ; Los Angeles County Museum of Art, Resnick Pavilion : 4,789 mL ; Hammer Museum : 4,139 mL ; Resnick Center for Food Law and Policy at UCLA School of Law : 4,039 mL). 2018 work in situ, completed 2019. Courtesy of artist and Visitor Welcome Center.

"WHAT THE EARTH SHALL YIELD": THE SYRIAN WAR, SEEDBANKS, AND THE COMING APOCALYPSE

MAUD DOYLE

At the End of Days, the Antichrist, al-Dajjal, will come to Syria astride a donkey, and he will walk the earth, converting people in marketplaces. Or he will come to Persia, with one blind eye "like a floating grape," and he will raise your loved ones from the dead. The world will be consumed by famine. Skies will withhold water, and not a living creature will be left on earth. But on al-Dajjal's command it will rain, and mountains of bread will block the intersections. The best of believers will be tempted, for he'll walk in a world made unbearable by human infractions, in which women work alongside men and men dye their hair; animal skins are used as carpets, interest is taken, and ill-gotten gains fund the building of tall buildings; men bear witness to what they did not witness, and affairs of state are managed by fools.

Three months before ISIS conquered Dabiq in Syria in 2014, promising to hasten the triumphant drums of Judgment Day, a gene bank 50 miles to the south of the town mailed 116,000 seed samples to Svalbard in Norway, the mythically impregnable seed bank located high in the North Atlantic, for safekeeping during the war. The bank, the International Center for Agricultural Research in the Dry Areas (ICARDA), had also been transferring their seed archives to two of their satellite research bases in Morocco and Lebanon, beyond the reach of the violence. Eighteen months later, ISIS was in power in Dabiq, and Russia had bombed Homs, the Doomsday clock, operated by *Bulletin of the Atomic Scientists*, inched two minutes closer to midnight, and ICARDA ordered a withdrawal of several thousand of their seeds from Svalbard to furnish their new research centers with genetic material, and perhaps put off the very apocalypse that pressed in around them.

It marked the first time, and way ahead of schedule, that the seed vault had been opened. A small hailstorm of headlines followed this bank order: "Syrian War Spurs First Withdrawal from Doomsday Arctic Seed Vault"; "Arctic 'Doomsday Vault' opens to retrieve vital seeds for Syria"; "Apocalypse Now"; "See the 'Doomsday' Seed Vault Opened in Response to Syria Crisis," was *National Geographic*'s chillingly voyeuristic angle. It almost seemed as though the vault had contained Gog and Magog themselves, and they were now hurtling through the air toward Aleppo (in fact, the seeds were sedately making their way to the new gene banks in Lebanon and Morocco). In the papers at least, it appeared that, woken from its slumber at last by the war in Syria, Doomsday had, quite suddenly, arrived.

At the time, an interviewer, on behalf of the Gregor Mendel Foundation, spoke to ICARDA's then-director, Mahmoud Solh. "Syria is one of the oldest cultural centers in the world, and especially with regard to modern farming," she said. "Are you afraid that all of this will be gone when you come back?" As if this war, rather than the innumerable other conflicts that have swept through Syria — not to mention the rest of the world — in the last several thousands of years, might finally spell the end of all that human innovation. It is touching almost, the breathless anticipation of this era's particular significance. "Is it not late? A late time to be living?" asks Annie Dillard in *For the Time Being*. "Our century and its unique Holocaust, its refugee populations, its serial totalitarian exterminations?" To think of ourselves instead as alive at no particular point, orbiting in an ongoing cycle without meaning or end, is inconceivable. "Who can bear to hear this?"

Long before the arrival of Doomsday headlines, a 1973 study forecast devastating food shortages in the Middle East; it was in response to this early warning that ICARDA was first established in Lebanon in 1977. In the face of Lebanese civil war, ICARDA relocated to Syria, where their geneticists and breeders have since quietly gone about their work. Their seeds, cryogenically frozen in 141,000 individual packets at 20 degrees Celsius, were routinely pulled out of cold storage by geneticists and planted in the surrounding farmland of Tal Hadya, a fertile region occupied by Syrian rebels since 2013. When the war broke out, they were searching — among their vast frozen archive of lentils, wheat, barley, fava beans, and a growing store of peas — for seeds that contained a natural resistance to a virulent wheat stem rust whose spores had been detected blowing over Africa and West Asia, just as they had blown through the Bible. (To stave off the rust and its attendant famines, ancient Romans sacrificed red animals; the same rust destroyed more than 20 percent of America's wheat crop several times between 1917 and 1935.) If they found resistant traits, these could be bred into new varieties of wheat, in order that the crops might resist the rust at the source.

At the beginning of Syria's unconscionable war, the gene bank's staff began evacuating their seeds, driving truckloads of them to Lebanon and Turkey along the back roads. International staff and others were advised to leave Syria when the fighting neared Aleppo in 2012, and 100 local technicians were left to operate a facility that had been run by 435. In 2014, the conflict approached Tal Hadya itself. ICARDA's trucks and generators began to disappear in the dark. Their fat-tailed Awassi sheep, bred to produce more milk and require less water, were hunted and eaten. The area around the station fell under the control of two competing militias, and the staff suffered two kidnappings. Despite these tribulations, between the springs of 2012 and 2014 the remaining staff managed the Svalbard deposit, duplicating 80 percent of their seed collection and shipping it off to Norway.

According to today's agro-scientists, the seeds sleeping in ICARDA's walk-in freezers represent the most plausible defense against hunger we have — against the shifting growing seasons, temperatures, and ecosystems; the growing frequency and variety of pestilence; the nearly 11 billion people expected to inhabit the earth in 2100; the exhausted soil; the loss of water; the rising tides; the dust. Land degradation and climatic changes have made the Middle East home to the world's most significant food deficits, and Syria and Jordan, barring immediate and significant changes, are expected to lose 30 percent of arable land to desertification. (One in seven people in the world could be displaced between now and 2050 by climate change, with the Middle East and North Africa understood to be the epicenter of the crisis.) The genetic traits that line ICARDA's shelves should enable breeders and geneticists to create more resistant, more productive crops that thrive in conditions in which agriculture has never before been tested.

The End Times, with their promise to upend the status quo, are often exploited as a call to arms. The first issue of Islamic State's notorious English-language recruitment rag, *Dabiq*, calls forth the apocalypse as related in the hadith — the vast sea of fragments of things the prophet is said to have said — of *Sahih Muslim*: "Abu Hurayrah reported that God's Messenger (*sallallahu 'alayhi wa sallam*) said, 'The Hour will not be established until the Romans land at al-A'maq or Dabiq,'" and an army from Medina will ride out to meet them in battle. (The reprinted account leaves out the prophet's warning, recorded in the same chapter of *Muslim*, that "⌊w⌋hen two Muslims face one another with their swords, both the slayer and the slain will be in fire." For recruitment purposes, the emphasis on conquest over peace is sufficient.)

This quotation is followed by a section titled "A new era has arrived of might and dignity for the Muslims." The spread features a testimonial from ISIS's second-in-command at the time, the late

Shaykh Abu Muhammad al-'Adnani, who wrote,

> The time has come for those generations that were drowning in oceans of disgrace [...] after their long slumber in the darkness of neglect — the time has come for them to rise. The time has come for the Ummah of Muhammad (*sallallahu 'alayhi wa sallam*) to wake up from its sleep, remove the garments of dishonor, and shake off the dust of humiliation and disgrace, for the era of lamenting and moaning has gone, and the dawn of honor has emerged anew. [...] Triumph looms on the horizon. The signs of victory have appeared.

It is tempting to read accounts of the apocalypse not only as an end to the chaos we call history, but as a story about going home, a return to the divine garden from which we were cast. The Apocalypse appeals because it promises the redress of insufferable wrongs. Victims become conquerors, the powerless are granted a starring role, and the irresolvable traumas of living tip toward rectification.

Eschatological foreboding abounds everywhere these days, but it resonates particularly in the war zones of West and Central Asia. The doomsday invoked by ISIS's strategists received a great deal more attention than the drought ravaging Mesopotamia and North Africa, but both correspond to a resurgence of apocalyptic feeling across the region. In the 2006 war between Israel and Lebanon, soldiers claimed afterward that they had seen the Mahdi on his white horse, charging Israeli tanks with his sword. Six years later, in the wake of the Arab Spring and the American withdrawal from Iraq, a Pew survey found that 72 percent of Muslim Iraqis and 83 percent of Muslim Afghanis expected to see the coming of the Mahdi in their lifetime. The figures were only slightly lower elsewhere in the region — only in Jordan, Palestine, and Egypt did the number of expectant dip below half the Muslim population.

After all, the signs are in place: drought, hunger, a battle with Jews in Jerusalem, the rule of tyrants, the burning of Yemen, war between Muslims in what is now Syria and Iraq (and now Turkey), a broader war of nations. Revelations of the Hour are most numerous — and most alive in the popular imagination — at moments when life has become unlivable. Apocalyptic narratives often arrive treading on the trains of minor tragedies — catastrophes on a human rather than cosmic scale. These stories constitute the narratives' frame, and then those hardships, manmade or predestined, spread like curls of smoke until the whole world is darkened by calamity.

The history of imminent apocalypses is ironically long, though many of the preceding texts, too, take place in what is now called the Middle East. The Apocalypse of Daniel, the first known example of the genre, has been placed in the Hellenistic Levant or Persia sometime in the second century BC and invokes Ephesus, Babylon, and Byzantium (this one is a real barnburner in which a beast has 10 horns that represent 10 kings, each of whom will be overthrown by an 11th horn, which appears suddenly and without explanation). Revelation features seven churches in the holy cities of West Asia and, of course, the Whore of Babylon. The action of 4

Sabrina Ratté, *BIOME III* from Biomes series, 2017, video HD, courtesy of the artist.

Ezra, which moves from a bedchamber to a psychedelic poppy field where Ezra has visions and sleeps for days, is thought to take place in and around Babylon as well, where the Jewish community lived in exile; the Byzantine apocalypses of the sixth and seventh centuries, self-evidently, take place in Constantinople. Perhaps it's natural that the birthplace of agriculture, writing, and civilization at large, with all its attendant ills, should also herald its end. "Years of drought will drive them, until they will be with you in your houses," reads a hadith collected in Nu'aym ibn Hammad's *Kitab al-fitan*, the book of tribulations, forecasting the migration crisis. "They will say, 'How long it is that we have hungered while you were satisfied?'"

In some texts, it is God who orchestrates man's descent from pure faith, while in others it seems the End might have been avoided by adequate repentance, at least for a while. Either way, God's eventual arrival on the scene, and the impending restoration of a just and ordered world of the faithful, is foreordained. He will come bearing a resolution to the contingencies of history, sweeping up the mess we've made of Eden.

If the rise of the genre and its persistence through history is any indication, the belief that life can't go on as it is may be wired into human experience of trauma and hardship. There must be something else that comes next, something gentler and more just, and so we keep one half-wary, half-hopeful eye on the horizon.

There is, however, a new twist in this old plot: the secularism of the Enlightenment encouraged the removal of God from the apocalyptic equation, placing divine power squarely in the hands of men, and that dictate still holds in the scientific community. Since at least the 19th century, seed banks and botanic gardens have been compared to arks, a refuge that would preserve humanity's agricultural accomplishments from the metaphorical flood. "It was hoped that the plants that had been scattered at the Fall might be gathered together again," wrote Richard Drayton wrote in 1996, "Europe thereby securing cures for disease and hunger and, perhaps, a reconciliation with the Creator." Perhaps unknowingly, Drayton echoed Qur'anic scripture, in which the arrival of Judgment Day is marked by the approach of the divine garden of plenty: "When the Garden has drawn near, then each soul will know what it has readied" (81:13–14).

Geneticists love to remember the heroism of the Vavilov Institute of Plant Industry, one of the world's oldest seed banks, whose glazed windows look out on St. Isaac's Square in St. Petersburg. In the winter of 1941, when the Nazis blockaded Leningrad and St. Petersburg starved, the scientists of the Vavilov Institute smuggled duplicate seeds out of the city, away from danger, to hide them in the Urals. In the grimy, imperial halls of the seed bank itself, the scientists who stayed to guard the collection voluntarily starved to death, martyrs surrounded by thousands of peanuts.

Agriculture is an anthropologist's genesis story. Agriculture's inception is located, like Eden, between the Tigris and Euphrates, at the end of the Pleistocene, when the ice began to recede and the temperatures began to warm, and the number of humans on earth increased. The Natufians first swung their flint sickles somewhere in the Levant, sometime between 12,500 and 10,000 BC gathering, wild barley. The Epipaleolithic people east of the Fertile Crescent began to raise the wild sheep and goats they had hunted. Rye, lentils, and vetch were gathered and slowly domesticated along the Euphrates Valley of Syria. In 8,500 BC, einkorn wheat was domesticated in Turkey. By 8,000 BC, the people of southwest Asia were dependent on agriculture.

The turning points of agricultural development are also the tipping points of some of the great human tragedies. On Columbus's return to America, in 1493, he brought with him the seeds of foreign plants — wheat, millet, onions, melon, grapes — and he returned to Spain with seeds native to the New World — corn, tomatoes, potatoes, squash. Agriculture became both the means and end of empire. Arab people domesticated coffee from Ethiopia and introduced it to India, where the Dutch acquired it, and cultivated it in Java. The British planted the Andean cinchona tree in India; the quinine from its bark was used for malarial treatment, which in turn enabled their colonization of Africa. In the United States, the siren promises of a planting a new Eden in the desert west inspired Americans to fulfill the call of Manifest Destiny and its attendant decimation of native populations. In Korea, French Indochina, the Philippines, Mexico, the US government wielded high-yield hybrid seeds on the agrarian front of its campaign against the Red Spread, leading to global monocultures.

Each innovation, in its turn, leads to an attendant catastrophe: decimation of North and South American indigenous peoples, slavery in the West Indies, the brutalization of Africa and the massacre of its people, global warming, and the loss of the genetic diversity we need to combat it. As in the scripture, the satisfaction of immediate returns transforms, through avarice, into an evil force, an Antichrist who promises mountains of bread and will ultimately damn us all.

And yet, geneticists still argue that agriculture and seed banks are the only means to achieve equality, and thereby salvation. In an urgently worded plea for action and investment in the *Guardian*, Solh warned European leaders about the disastrous implications of climate change in the Middle East. Drought, food shortages, insects, and pestilence, he wrote, will breed a tribe of political disasters on a global scale: poverty, mass migration, civil unrest, catastrophic youth unemployment and its lurking co-conspirator, extremism. "As long as such conditions prevail, these areas will remain 'soft targets' for extremist organisations," writes Solh. "We need to recognize this migration crisis as the canary in the mine." This version of putting off the apocalypse is, in a way, the exact inverse of ISIS's (or 12th century Byzantium's) eagerness to invite it: either use the specter of the Hour to summon recruits to epic battle or use it to develop industries that can make epic battle less appealing. The more bearable the act of living can be made, the less need to rush toward its conclusion. Writes Solh: "The long-term solution is clear: give rural people the ability to remain productive and employed in their own settings."

In Australia, in the Western and Midwestern United States, in sub-Saharan and Northern Africa, the Middle East, Central Asia, and other regions of formerly fertile land, dry areas have turned hotter and drier, droughts have grown more frequent and more extreme. Agro-scientists expect that soon enough, all of these landscapes will resemble the water-scarce steppes of Syria. The majority of seed samples from ICARDA's Morocco satellite — on average 20,000 a year — go to researchers right here at home, like Kansas State University and the University of North Dakota.

That we could potentially put off the apocalypse with the eschatological preparations of a handful of prophetic scientists is just a variation on eschatological faith. News outlets and researchers alike have gladly appropriated the language of the apocalypse to talk about rising seas and winds made of dust, recognizing that the drama of four horsemen can engage a wider readership than incremental temperature increases, no matter how devastating. "Saving seeds is not as sexy as say, saving the dolphins," laments *National Geographic*. Scientists are betting that the urgency of an impending end will, like an approaching deadline, enable change, that perhaps desperation can make survival possible.

The Islamic tradition's end times, like all others, unfurl in endless variation, but also like others — though perhaps less overtly — the world often doesn't actually end. The word apocalypse comes from the Greek word *apokalupsis*, meaning *to reveal*, or more literally, *to uncover*. Technically, "The Apocalypse of John" refers to his description of the future, not his prediction of our demise. Over and over again, what the texts seem to predict is often further revelation, more scripture. Hadith say that Christ will fly down from heaven to kill al-Dajjal with his spear, and "he will dissolve […] as aloes dissolve when the sun hits them." This is followed by seven or eight years of peaceful rule by the Mahdi, but even this is only the middle of the end, to be followed by a promise described as "a divine shout" against which believers can stop up their ears and live, though they may envy the dead, who at least got to hear what the shout had to say. We may wish our era to be significant, but as climate scientists and others calling for urgent action have found, we often seem unable to contemplate the true end of human life, and perhaps we never really have.

All the great monotheisms' apocalypses give an account of the descent of the world from righteousness into entropy, and all of them end with a promise: Revelation predicts a gem-encrusted Jerusalem, forbidden to all fornicators; Sura 81 of the Qur'an promises a garden of such sustenance that all want is eliminated; the (apocryphal) Jewish apocalypse called 4 Ezra promises the revelation of 70 hidden books of scripture written with a tongue of fire that contain, presumably, answers to some urgent and unnamable question, perhaps the very question that compels us toward the End. "I, Salathiel, who am also called Ezra," it begins:

> I was troubled as I lay on my bed, and my thoughts welled up in my heart, because I saw the desolation of Zion and the wealth of those who live in Babylon […] And now, oh Lord, why have you handed [your chosen people] over to the many, and dishonored your one root beyond the others, and scattered [us]?"

The final image reverberates: a people uprooted and scattered like seeds.

ICARDA's withdrawal from Svalbard faded from the news as suddenly as it had come. It enabled ICARDA to stock their research centers in Morocco and Lebanon, and the agricultural Doomsday loomed, once again, in a more distant future. Saving the seeds is not as sexy as saving the world.

For a time, the station at Tal Hadya remained operational, even after it had been seized by rebels belonging to the Salafist coalition Ahrar al-Sham in 2015. It turned out that the leader of the group was a farmer, and the rebels and geneticists struck a deal: in exchange for food and power, the rebels promised protection to local farmers who would continue the work of the research farm and keep the generators running. Ahmed Amri, the head of ICARDA's genetic resources unit, gave an interview at the time to an environmental news magazine. "We're very lucky that the rebels realize the importance of conserving biodiversity; it's one of the activities that has never been interrupted in Aleppo," he said. "But we cannot predict how each day will be." The following year, when the Bashar al-Assad's forces began targeting Tal Hadya, much of the remaining staff packed up the remaining samples and left for Lebanon. The operation of the facility and the farms fell to the employees without the means to leave.

ICARDA deposited duplicates of the seeds they had withdrawn from Svalbard in 2017. The action was hailed as a success which proved that, in the words of ICARDA's current director general, "we can get one step closer to a food-secure world." And yet, in January, the *Bulletin* made its annual assessment of global stability, and, citing nuclear proliferation and climate change, moved the Doomsday Clock closer to midnight than it had been since the 1950s. "The [*Bulletin*] today sets the Doomsday Clock at two minutes to midnight," read the accompanying statement, "the closest it has ever been to apocalypse."

ICARDA headquarters' relocation to Lebanon is a testament to the circular nature of history: the organization is back where it was founded over 30 years ago. Its headquarters once again spread out at the bottom of Bekaa Valley, in Terbol. The square tents of a Syrian refugee camp unfold outside the city, and along the highways fly the green flags, emblazoned with a yellow AK-47, of Hezbollah, to which the valley is also home. Orchards and vineyards have dominated the valley since it served as the breadbasket to Rome's Levantine empire in the first century BC, and the basin remains a tessellation of greens and golds. The white greenhouses of ICARDA arc in a quiet, orderly row near the station, shadows stretching long as their pale skins flush blue in the evening, while fields of emerald, chartreuse, and viridian quiver at the base of purpling hills. Muhammad councils, according to *Muslim*, that "[i]f the last hour comes while you have a palm cutting in your hands and it is possible to plant it before the Hour comes, you should plant it."

Sabrina Ratté, *Radiances I*, 2017, Video HD, courtesy of the artist

DARK WAS THE NIGHT, COLD WAS THE GROUND

J.D. DANIELS

"My poor son, that friend of yours is an idiot," my father said to me when Bloch had gone. "My goodness! He can't even tell me what the weather's like! Why, nothing is more interesting!" — Proust

Early last night there was a ring around the moon. Low and burning yellow, it peered at us through trees. If you were not disposed to see a burning yellow eye in a gauzy halo, you might instead have seen light refracting through ice crystals in translucent cirrostratus clouds: a warm front was climbing over cold air from behind, pushing higher, cooling and condensing. "It's going to rain," my girlfriend said, and that was true. All night and the next morning was a wet mess.

1.

Nick was the first person I told I was leaving my wife. That's not exactly right. First, I told my girlfriend. Then I told Nick. Then I told my wife. I called him and said we had to go to the desert, and he said okay. On my way to Logan Airport by yellow cab, I saw a coyote standing in the middle of an empty soccer field, looking glum.

I transferred at Denver and flew over the Rockies, headed for McCarran International. The three girls in their gray hooded college sweatshirts seated behind me were smashing back drinks and couldn't seem to decide whether they wanted to hand in all their money at once or lose it bit by bit over the coming week.

"Woo, bitches," one of them said, and another said, "Woo."

A long silence and the turning of magazine pages. Then: "Vegas, bitches."

One of the girls said, "What if we start with a shot of our feet? And you say, 'Woo.' Then the camera pulls out and I say, 'Bitches.'"

"Girl, you swear too much."

"Nay, bitches."

"Girl, that's just what I mean."

"'Bitches' isn't swearing. 'Bitches' is just *bitches*."

"Ladies and gentlemen," the intercom said, "the pilot has illuminated the 'fasten your seatbelts' sign."

"Woo, bitches," one of the girls said.

Nick and I rented a car and got out of Vegas. I stared through the window of our Ford Focus at that huge expanse of red rock. In Utah, everything's hundreds of miles away and you have to drive forever, getting it on, you know, really doing it, motorvating, pedal to the metal, hell-bent for leather, before you get nowhere. The country's so good to look at that when night falls, it's a relief. It's so beautiful it hurts to see.

We drove through a dark tunnel more than a mile long under a red mountain. It was not a geological feature and not a feat of engineering, it was something a man might dream. We came out of that tunnel into brilliant sunshine in Zion, Utah. White-tailed deer, jackrabbits, a vole scuttling, come in under the shadow of this red rock. We checked in at the ranger station. They expected an inch or two of precipitation overnight, they said. We got our back-country passes. We parked at the trailhead and changed into our snowpants and boots. We strapped on our packs and hiked miles and miles in, post-holing through the occasional field of hip-deep snow.

I had never seen so many different kinds of country in one day. Ankle-deep, boot-sucking mud. Sand. Scat with hair in it, remnants shat out by some meat-shitting meat-eater. Green trees ringed with fallen blue berries. More trees, burnt twisted and black. Trees beavers had gnawed to points on either end, and the creek they'd dammed.

And all around us in the ravines were sky-high canyon walls; and all around us when we were up on the spines, high on the ridges, were blue vistas so far-ranging they made me sweat.

We made our camp. I zipped myself into a graded-for-below-freezing sleeping bag still wearing my long underwear, silks top and bottom, a T-shirt, three long-sleeved shirts, a fleece vest, a down jacket, a waterproof rust-orange windbreaker, another pair of long underwear bottoms with red-and-brown woodpecker stripes, wool socks, a pair of gloves, and a black balaclava. I wanted to stay warm.

Night fell and with it rain came, swelling the nearby creek. The tent leaked and our boots, sitting outside the tent, filled with water, and the trail flooded as the rain turned to sleet before the sleet turned to snow, obliterating our flooded-out trail. We woke in the dark under three feet of snow with snow still falling.

We rummaged in one of the packs for a roll of toilet paper and we squatted and grunted in the snow, in the dark. Every minute the snow got deeper and the trail, by now nothing more than a suggestion in the snow, became still fainter, more and more obscure. "Hmm," Nick said. Then he said, "Fuck."

Our leisurely three-and-a-half-hour hike in became an eight-hour march out through still deepening snow, checking the compass, looking at the bottoms of our boots to see if we had stepped in the red dirt of the trail under all that snow, cutting trail where we couldn't find the trail, bushwhacking, sloshing through creeks waist-deep where crossing on the smooth rocks was foolhardy because if we had to sleep in the goddamn park another goddamn night we would only be hungry, angry, and uncomfortable, whereas if our sleeping bags got wet we would freeze to death, getting lost and turning back around, pushing snow, staying warm because hiking was hard enough work to make us sweat through our coats.

We didn't talk much. Once, looking at geologic eons in a striated red rock wall, Nick said, "Lately the forms of things appear to me with time one of their visible dimensions." It's Robinson Jeffers.

God, I said to God, when I get back to Massachusetts, if I ever do, I will never complain about shoveling snow again. Instead, I will say these words: I have been to the snow-making factory, where they make the snow, and I took the tour. I mumbled this prayer, or bargain.

"What are you saying?" Nick said.

"In my mind I am drafting a letter of commendation," I said, "about how your competence and tenacity got us out of this canyon."

"Not yet," Nick said. Then he fell.

He slid only about 10 feet, but hit his knee on a rock. I can't carry him out of here, I thought. I guess I can if I have to. I waited, but he didn't move.

I said, "Are you hurt?"

"That hurt," he said, "but I'm not hurt."

I made my way down to him. "Can you walk?" I said.

He stood up. "We'll find out," he said.

About the time we'd had enough, only halfway out of the canyon but already running on fumes, Nick and I ran into five shivering college kids from Michigan. Real kids, young enough to be our sons, if the pregnancy scare Erica and I'd had in 1992 had been even scarier. They had packed in two tents, a pair of snowshoes, an acoustic guitar, a bag of sandwiches, and a gallon of vodka. They knew we'd gone farther into the back country than they had, they'd seen us on our way in the day before and they had waited for us to pass their campsite and cut a trail for them to follow. They were hungover, lost and helpless, abashed. Now we had something to pity other than our dumb selves.

One of them, gap-toothed and sandy blond, drew near me to indicate that he understood the gravity of his predicament.

"Bit off more than we could chew," he said. "Thank God for you guys. Where you from?"

Satoshi Kojima, *Weather Report*, 2016, oil on canvas, 66 7/8 x 90 1/2 inches.
Image copyright Satoshi Kojima, courtesy of the artist, Bridget Donahue, New York, and TRAMPS, New York.

"Kentucky. Then Boston."

"I'm from Grand Rapids, if you know it."

"My wife was from Grand Rapids," I said.

He didn't have anything to say about that. "You hike this canyon before?" he said.

"No."

"Me neither. Mother Zion is angry with us."

I can't tolerate that crap, *Mother This* and *Mother That*. We kept walking.

"Yeah," he said, trying again. "First time."

"It could cure you," I said.

When they spotted their van at last, on the trailhead across the final decline and grueling ascent, one of the kids threw his hands up and yelled, "Spring Break!"

"Woo, bitches," I said to Nick.

After nine hours of it we were back in the Ford, slopping red mud in its floorboards, shouting along with Joe Cocker hollering *Ain't it high time we went?* and quietly agreeing as Roy Orbison confessed *She's a mystery to me.* We stopped for gas and ate tacos and steaks and enchiladas and coffee. We didn't have a lot to say to each other.

In our motel in Flagstaff, below the snow-line, we ordered General Tso's chicken and hot and sour soup and fried rice and Mongolian beef and Crab Rangoon. I got up in the night to piss and, forgetting that I couldn't walk, stumbled and fell into the television. There's some folks who will tell you that I am still in that motel room, holding my head, sitting on the carpeted floor.

2.

Years later, when, over the winter of 2014–'15, Boston had more than 100 inches of snow, breaking the all-time record, I cheered for more. We're so close to the record, come on, let's get it on. We got five feet of snow in February alone.

It became normal to be notified that 20 inches were expected over night. "Today's headlines: panic and buy shit," I said to Marc, the owner of the corner grocery, and he smirked. He was making a lot of money. Panic is big business.

A crippling and possibly historic blizzard, the language of advertising. "It's the crippler!" James said, and we laughed, recalling what Russell used to say about getting with girls back in school. *I slipped her the crippler*, he said.

But the truth is I was nervous. Three feet of snow, power outages, I'd bought a snow-throwing machine and my neighbors were counting on me. I had started snorting benzodiazepines when I thought no one was looking. They were looking, though.

Our hot water shut down. The furnace began to leak. I was shoveling for an hour, then reading *Grammar of Akkadian* for an hour: I'd been given permission to audit the course. I shoveled, then I listened to Sonny Criss's "The Black Apostles" before I shoveled some more. I did two shifts with the snow-thrower and snorted half a pill I chopped up with the edge of a nail-file, I thought I was so smart. I flagged a city plow down out on the main drag and paid him cash to come down our dead-end street. He pushed the snow high enough to block my neighbor David's kitchen window.

Another foot of snow. I cleared the window-well, the furnace vent, and the gas meter. I shoveled the stairs to the basement: without enough clearance over my head to pitch the snow out of the well, I had to fill and refill a plastic bin and haul it up the stairs and dump it out back. I cleared both downspouts. I chipped off the undercarriage-scraping ice-block that had formed at the mouth of our street: while I did that, a man walked out in his robe and house-shoes to stare at his Honda Civic: plowed in along the main drag, now frozen solid under feet of dirty ice.

Another foot of snow. Concerned about flooding when and if the melt began, I shoveled the storm drain clean: used the long-handled ice-chipper until I could see iron and concrete, then worked on my hands and knees with a paint-scraper, getting lost in the details until it was one hundred percent ice-free, and finally heated kettle after kettle on the stove-top and poured two gallons of scalding water over and into the grate.

Another foot of snow. Night after freezing night, I dreamt of Death Valley, where in 1913 this temperature had been recorded: 134 degrees Fahrenheit, in the shade. *Death Valley is full of flowers*, my dream said.

At night, I stood on the brick terrace in the dark, in the deep snow. I wasn't in danger; I could call for help, and friends would come running: I was close enough to see the lights of Erik and Traci's house, and Arthur and Jane's house, and David and Judy's house, and Bill's house, and Brenda's house.

But I looked at the stars, remembering Zion, and I trembled.

Sabrina Ratté, *BIOME II* from Biomes series, 2017, video HD, courtesy of the artist.

Alexandre Dorriz, *Untitled Wormhole 06*, 2018, Sony MiniDV Camcorder, Stainless Steel Nails, Exposed Silk (2 Silkworm Cocoons exposed to YouTube search algorithm, "9/11 videos"played continually for 10 days), Needle. 4 x 6 x 8 inches.

POLISTES CAROLINA

A.H. JERRIOD AVANT

I avoid heat   by choosing cooler
sides of sliding glass doors. I

am as untouchable   as any ghost
cut off from the one who waits

to prove its horrific lineage and
name I reserve. The weather woman

reports a heat index of 105 by noon
and beyond the reaches of ample

light   thirteen or fourteen hang
and stand post outside their home

built onto our home. Hare-footed
they clutter above passageways. They

red-bodied   black-winged and deft
more precise than anything this mean

breathing   and they itch to come ruin
parts of our small   country. Inverted

they loll   in untroubled ways   and I
want to feed them flakes of their own

wings. I slide glass to neutralize the
small but fast and fiery threat. I beg

only corpses to outlast their living.
Count the screwed bodies I've

gathered   with forefingers around
the necks of toxic cannisters.

When the nest falls   I exhale until
my cheeks balloon   in relief that

I've left the nest   too wet to continue
to hang. I am the killer their house

is unable to make and I get away
with a hot throne   of shallow graves

dripping at the edges   of my feet.

Latefa Noorzai, *Untitled (LN 182)*, 2018, Acrylic on paper, 30 x 22.5 inches.

ERAVAMO NOI

MOLLY PRENTISS

I was at war with the brands, but I was working for the brands. In those days, you couldn't not. They were start-up denims and neoprene wearables and click caps and cloud spaces. Their offerings had leaked out into the air, as if through a sleek diffuser.

I was deeply involved with the brands at the same time as I was punishing myself for being involved with the brands. I was trying to spit them out but instead I was breathing them in. On any given day you could find me in front of my screen, selling myself as I sold things for the brands. What I did was tell stories for the brands, about the brands. Urban best practice new dream girl retinol direct to consumer love stories that would sit in designated squares of the Shopify site. And then the nylon zip flap bungee rig was born. And that's how the unstoppable shoelace monitor came to be. And that's how we knew there was an opening in the marketplace — we spotted it from a million miles away like a mirage in a desert — which we had originally believed to be devoid of openings but which we only had to look at harder to see what we saw: the squiggly rainbows of opportunity signaling to us from a distance, drawing us ever-nearer.

I walked toward the rainbow and I cringed. I was at war with the brands in the way that I could be at war with my own body or face, how I saw it in the mirror and could so easily identify the flaws, the bad sag, the largeness that was also smallness, the dents the world had made, the transparent skin. But I couldn't do anything about it, I couldn't advance any troops for it would be useless and I knew it. The human body, like the social body, had a mind of its own, and so it was a quiet war, a cold war, a war of threats never acted upon, of almost uprooting it all but never uprooting it all, eventually finding my way back into the original predicament.

It was hard work, the work I did for the brands. I had trouble with it because it wasn't how I naturally told stories. I naturally told stories in my own voice to my own friends, and I could back up or just stop entirely whenever I wanted, just make a joke and abort the whole mission altogether. But the stories I told for the brands had to be in the brand's voice — we liked to think of the brands as breathing, speaking things, because it made them less threatening — and for the brand's customers. I had never met the brand's actual customers. They were 35–40-year-old males with disposable incomes or 55–65-year-old females with disposable incomes. They had time enough to scroll and scroll and add to cart but not time enough to embody their personal desires without the help of the brands, who promised to help them do so. The brands were always making promises, which meant, of course, that I was making promises, as I was the one speaking for the brands in their voices. It was so worrisome, making promises you didn't know whether or not you could keep. Sometimes the worry ate me alive.

The worry almost did kill me once, eight or so months after I gave birth to my daughter. My daughter was a solid and funny baby, which was wonderful to witness, but motherhood had me on shaky ground. My mission statement had to change entirely from what it had once been. The "About" section was very different, too. I had to add "Mother" to my résumé, but no one accepted it as a legitimate position as it was not validated by an influential institution, which meant, of course, that my body was not an influential institution. One of the pillars for my personal brand voice had once been *confidence*, but that pillar started to crumble in front of my very eyes as I began to regard my resume and my body with a new skepticism. I became paralyzed for long stretches, sitting on the rug with my child. I was in love with her, and often brought her cheeks up to my mouth and kissed and kissed and kissed. The new pillars of my personal brand had become *sag*, *paralysis*, and *bedraggled feminine affection*.

At first, my immobilization felt like part of the deal: everyone gave you leeway when you were new at something. New Mother, as a brand, was strong and radiant while somehow maintaining a delicate sensuousness that people were attracted to and wanted to be part of. But when too much time passed, when the brand identity became dated, but the brand couldn't afford a site redesign, when New Mother slid into Should Have It Together By Now Mother, people weren't so quick to sign on. People stopped clicking on your home page, stopped coming to your home. Your child was messy and loud now, no longer a benign, sleeping lump. Yours alone to deal with, to discipline, to put to sleep, to decide to coddle or not. The loneliness of being a mother to a child that was too old to fall asleep on your body but too young to go to school was some of the strongest of all the brands of loneliness I had bought into. Stronger, even, than Pregnant Loneliness or Adolescent Loneliness or what I assumed Empty Nest loneliness would be like. Many times a week, I cried.

It was during this period when I began my war with the brands. Most things had become more confusing and muddled in motherhood — When was the best time to take a shower? At what intervals would I pump the milk from my body? Who should I give the largest parts of my love to? What were souls made of? — but a few select things became clearer. I began to understand the pointlessness of certain values and ways of being, and this unveiled itself first in relationship to the brands. Having a baby made me understand what creating life felt like, which in turn revealed to me its opposite: creating death. Which was what working for the brands was, if you thought about it in a certain way.

The written word, I had understood but not fully, could have an immense amount of power when wielded properly. This is why the brands wanted people like me: for our power. The power of the artists was different from the power of the non-artists because the power of the artists was emotional, by design. Emotion was our bread and butter. By using us, the brands could elicit emotional responses from their customers, which we all know are the responses that make us want to buy things or change things about ourselves (which leads, of course, to buying things). And so I used my ability and power to inhabit the minds and hearts of other people, or perhaps more accurately my ability to *imagine* the minds and hearts of other people, to deliver words that would stun or focus or please or prompt them, so that, presumably, they would purchase the object or service the brand was providing.

The object the brand was providing in this specific instance, the instance which spurred the war between myself and the brands, was made in Italy, a point which I touted in the Brand Story as one of its selling points. When something was made in Italy it was thought to be not only elegant but authentic, as if by purchasing it you could access a part of the Old World, a world in which people cared about quality in a way that they didn't in the New World. But the object the brand was providing, which was a purse, was made not by an Italian person but by a Chinese person, a young woman named Lin who had built, in Prato, Italy, from the ground up, a small factory out of which she sold textiles and leather goods manufactured by other Chinese people, one of whom was her daughter Ling. The fact that the purse was made by a Chinese person did not, of course, mean that it was a product of lesser quality than if it had been made by an Italian person, at least not necessarily, and yet I knew, as the brand knew, that it would not have been a selling point to say "Made by a Chinese Person in Italy" on the product's label or website. And so I did not write this.

Latefa Noorzai, *Untitled (LN 132)*, 2018, Acrylic on paper, 11x15 inches.

Lin had immigrated to Italy from Wenzhou when her daughter Ling was just four years old. She had come with an uncle who had a friend in Prato who'd already set up shop; he had rented a large warehouse which he'd turned into a factory, where Lin could work, making more money in a day than she'd make in Wenzhou in a week. This friend of Lin's uncle had tapped into a thriving business; he was importing very cheap fabrics from China and using the immigrant labor in Prato to churn out quickly and cheaply made garments. The European retail stores were eating it up, and though the local merchants were on his case for stealing their customer base — he'd had a fire extinguisher bashed through his car window once — he was proud of the business he was doing; it was proving to fill a niche that people wanted filled.

Lin worked in her uncle's friend's factory until Ling was 12, at which point she had saved up enough money and gained enough industrious conviction to cut herself loose and begin her own business. She wanted to work with leather — it was tough and soft at the same time, and she loved the smell, and she knew leather goods sold for much more than cheap textiles — and so she and Ling worked for a year at an Italian shoe factory, where they both learned the ins and outs of dealing with leather. On the evening they quit, they each ate a large bowl of noodles and Lin drank a large glass of wine and they grinned at each other over the dim table. Ling ordered her first shipment of leather the next morning, and it arrived at their apartment two weeks later. They began to make the purses I was supposed to write about now, which were now being sold at department stores in America.

The purses were beautiful in the way of many Italian things — they felt durable yet sensual, with appealingly impractical details. They were not difficult to write about. You could tell the story from a craftsmanship angle or from a fashion angle and both would improve the purse's chances of being sold. The purse was handmade with the most careful stitching, and you could wear it with the season's 1960s-inspired trench coats. The American woman who bought the purse that Ling and Lin created wanted only to be reassured that she was doing the right thing, nothing more. She was like a mother who, when letting her child out of the house in the evening, only wanted to be assured by the child that they would not ingest alcohol or drugs. As if the child's word meant anything when held up against her gargantuan fears of not being enough, of losing everything she loved most, of destruction, of withering, and perhaps most importantly, of her own obsolescence.

I wrote the story about the bag that this woman wanted to read. I told her everything was going to be okay, and that this bag would contribute to that okayness. By owning this bag, I promised her, she would feel worldly and worth it, plugged into her own womanhood, desirable, and more complete than she did currently. I wrote this story while my daughter was taking her naps — either the longer one in the morning or the sometimes nonexistent one in the evening, through which I tried to close my ears while she cried her way into her dreams. I had much anxiety while I wrote, but I couldn't tell where it was coming from exactly. I thought about my daughter in her crib and about the diaper subscription I had to renew, which cost me $76 every month, and how I needed to finish the story about the brand in order to afford the diaper subscription. I thought about Ling and Lin, and I wondered if Ling looked in at Lin while she slept sometimes, like I did often with my daughter, with a mixture of wonder and fear. I thought about Ling going out on the balcony of her apartment above the factory she'd built from scratch and smoking an Italian cigarette and looking down on the street, which was quiet except for a few teenage boys, riding their bikes into oblivion. And I thought about the old Italian woman who lived across the street from Ling's factory, who closed her shutters when she saw the glow of Ling's cigarette, though she had come to her own balcony to have a cigarette of her own.

The old woman, whose name was Giulia, had grown up on that street, her father had grown up on that street, and now it was Chinatown, everything was red and gold and very dirty. Gone were the people and things she knew, gone was her father, gone was her daughter who had moved to Rome and forgotten her, gone was her husband who had died before her, gone was her small dog Bruno who she'd let eat fish from her plate, and now she was all alone in the middle of a sea of foreigners; when she looked outside she found nothing she recognized. Where there had once been Italian leather workers there were now Chinese leather workers, and where there had once been an outdoor market there were now terrible clothes made of terrible materials blowing like slutty flags in the wind.

The old woman had thought, once, that she might befriend a Chinese person, either out of a kind of pity for the person or need to make her day to day existence less lonely, but when she had tried smiling at the woman who ran the factory in the garage across the street, the woman had scowled at her and rolled the grate of the garage down. Before the grate had closed she saw the woman's young daughter look at her pleadingly, and she thought of herself as a young girl, how her mother kept her inside to work in the kitchen when it was so beautiful outside, how she had watched her brothers bound through the fields and come back dirty and sunburned and flushed, waiting to be fed. She hated that woman across the street, for keeping her girl inside to work like that. She hated the Chinese people who had made her life so hellish and different. Who had made her life like a prison. Yet when her daughter had told her to come to Rome, she had declined. As she closed her shutters she felt angrier than ever before: her daughter had no idea what her life was, no respect for the past, no clue what it would mean to leave this street and pack up her things and go to Rome, where she would know no one at all, where she couldn't count on anything, not even her own distaste for the smell of steaming pork buns and leather that leaked into her living room every afternoon, which was when she knew she could open a bottle of wine and lift her first cigarette out of its silver case, the case that was once her grandmother's and now was hers.

My daughter woke up from her nap and I had to stop writing about the purses. I took the creaky stairs up to her bedroom, stood outside the door for a moment to hear if she was really awake or fake awake; sometimes she made noises in her sleep, which was always a relief, for then I could stay working longer. I was at war with myself about this feeling: wanting her, so desperately, to stay sleeping, to sleep as long and as much as possible, so that I could exist for longer periods of time inside of my own freedom. And yet I filled this freedom with brands, with work for the brands, every moment I was not with my daughter I was writing stories for the brands, which did not feel like freedom at all when I thought about it, and I would become angry with myself for the way I spent my time, the kind of woman I'd become, the woman who was angry with herself for how she spent her time and for the kind of woman she'd become.

I do not wish to be lazy, or to avoid work. That is not it. I do not wish that, as a human species, we could carry on without responsibility or task, lounging in the cloudy worlds of intellectualism or Buddhism or depression or dreams. I do not wish to sit on the floor with my daughter forever, trying in vain to entertain her while I drift away into my own mental universe. I am older now, not by much, but by some. My daughter is now three. I look at her and wonder what I can do. I fear the future with every bone in my body. I wait for her to become something abstract. She will develop her own voice, whose pillars I will only have control of in the same way I have control of a brand's; I can tell a story that people will believe, but it has a slim chance of being the correct one. I imagine her in Rome with sunglasses on. I imagine her swimming. I imagine her sitting in front of a computer, working alongside me, fighting my same silent war. I hear her again. She is awake. Here I come. Here I come, sweet girl. I am ready to plant myself in the earth so you can climb up me like a tree.

THE CALIFORNIA DESIGN DOMINION: THIRTEEN PROPOSITIONS

PETER LUNENFELD

In 1995, designer Andy Cameron and academic Richard Barbrook, both based in London, published a critique of the neoliberal order they saw emerging from the Golden State, almost 6,000 miles away. They labeled this constellation of digital technologies and free market ideas "The Californian Ideology." Barbrook and Cameron's opening paragraph laid out the terrain as they saw it:

> There is an emerging global orthodoxy concerning the relation between society, technology and politics. We have called this orthodoxy "the Californian Ideology" in honour of the state where it originated. By naturalising and giving a technological proof to a

> libertarian political philosophy, and therefore foreclosing on alternative futures, the Californian Ideologues are able to assert that social and political debates about the future have now become meaningless.

Looking at these ideas a quarter of a century later — after Google, Facebook, Snapchat, smartphones, and the merging of Silicon Valley tech and Hollywood content — we can see that this "orthodoxy" is no longer emerging, it is firmly established as the ubiquitous design template for 21st-century cultures, economies, and power relationships. Neoliberalism comes in many guises, and it adapts itself over time and across borders, shapeshifting to accommodate the local conditions. But what all the flavors share is a common recipe: start by financializing as many social and political relationships as possible, then add tax cuts for the wealthy and deregulation of business, stir in privatization of formerly public services and affordances, and finish off with an almost religious confidence that the "data" shows this dish is not just the best on the menu — it should be the only one on the menu.

As prescient as Barbrook and Cameron were, the geographic intelligence they offered about "California" was limited, perhaps as the result of their perspective from London — a very long way from the Pacific Coast. Barbrook and Cameron were seduced by Silicon Valley's own hype for itself, but did not understand that Northern and Southern California (always coastal, never inland) are a construct that complement and even demand each other's contributions and talents. One of Antonio Gramsci's most quoted lines both applies and has been superseded here: "The crisis consists precisely in the fact that the old is dying and the new cannot be born."

In California, the new was not so much born as designed, and what was "Designed in California" (to adopt the phrase that Apple plasters over its Chinese-made products) took over the whole world. We are no longer in the realm of ideology but instead under what I call "dominion," a version of empire that does not rely on military power so much as a sense of shared culture. We've seen this before: as their empire contracted in the 20th century, the British experimented with alternate concepts, and at the Imperial Conference of 1926 offered "dominion," defined as "autonomous communities [...] equal in status united by a common allegiance" for Canada, Australia, New Zealand, and South Africa. California extends its global dominion in a similar "cultural" way not via boots on the ground or even ballots in the box, but rather via design and its seductions. The California Design Dominion is a market populism, an opaque form of control supported with every post liked, software updated, or entertainment streamed. We also shouldn't discount the religious connotations of the word, which come from a famous passage of Genesis 1:28. "And God blessed them, and God said unto them, Be fruitful, and multiply, and replenish the earth, and subdue it: and have dominion over the fish of the sea, and over the fowl of the air, and over every living thing that moveth upon the earth." This dominion can either be interpreted as a call for conscious stewardship, or as unfettered license to exploit. Either and both interpretations work for the California Design Dominion.

The California Design Dominion deploys everything from interface to user experience to narrative arcs to fuse two 19th-century concepts: the utopianism of the *Gesamtkunstwerk* and the pragmatism of "commercial art." Out of that fusion, it has created a globalized, techno-economic culture that spans the globe. The California Design Dominion manifests across a huge range of disciplines, but what unifies them is the way they square the circle of empowering individuals to "free" information while simultaneously devising ways to monetize the flow of information. One of the key factors of the California Design Dominion is that no matter how much it appears to celebrate "disruptors," "innovators," "rebels," and "unicorns," it's very much invested in making sure that those who arrive first get the majority of the spoils. In other words: It's Settler Colonialism 2.0.

That neoliberal, settler colonialist mindset was enacted into California state law in 1978 by a Los Angeles anti-tax activist named Howard Jarvis, who pushed through what he called "the People's Initiative to Limit Property Taxation." Sold as a mechanism to protect the elderly from being forced from their homes by unsustainable tax increases, the law — which has become the untouchable third rail of state politics — instead ensured that the richest generation of Californians ever, the beneficiaries of a trillion-dollar infusion of federal investment into the state, would never be asked to give back to the state in any meaningful way. There were racial and cultural components to the campaign, with the white population using the vote as a way to pull up the drawbridge before the emerging diverse majority could benefit from the largesse that had supported the growth of the state up until the mid-'70s. The law is best known as "Proposition 13" and it helped to usher in the era of conservatism, austerity, and neoliberalism that is now identified with Ronald Reagan in the United States and Margaret Thatcher in the United Kingdom. What follows are 13 propositions about the California Design Dominion that followed in their wake.

PROPOSITION 1: California Is No Longer a Simulation of Anything

When Barbrook and Cameron wrote their essay, it was still an intellectual commonplace to claim that California was a "simulation." The lords of deconstruction and hyperreality like Jacques Derrida and Jean Baudrillard were regular visitors to University of California campuses during the 1970s and '80s, particularly the new campus in suburban Irvine. In his interview with L.A. free jazz pioneer Ornette Coleman, Derrida declared his method of blinkered geographical understanding: "This is always a conviction: we know ourselves by what we believe." Baudrillard's *America*, both a travelogue and a book of critical theory, posits California as the ultimate "'hysterical' simulation," the ultimate in hyperreality. This fascination goes hand in glove with a sense of suspicion. Christa Wolf, a novelist born in East Germany, was intrigued enough by her stay in Los Angeles to publish *City of Angels or, The Overcoat of Dr. Freud* in 2010 (the English translation came out in 2013) but she felt compelled to add the warning that the ocean in Southern California "has no smell," unlike the Baltic seas of her youth.

For all their Old World wit and continental insight, there is a sense that these temporary émigrés, or better yet, recurring visitors, bring to Southern California not an openness, but rather a closed sys-

Oscar Tuazon, *Los Angeles Water School*, 2018, images courtesy of LAND.

tem. They continue a centuries-old parlor game of looking at the New World and asking what had been missing or copied from their own environments. What was said of America in general applied even more so to the distillation of difference that was to them California. In their desire (*there's* a French concept that will never die) to dismiss the state, they missed the burgeoning reality that the rest of the world was becoming more like California rather than the other way around.

PROPOSITION 2: The Rest of the World Is a Skeuomorph of the Golden State

Skeuomorphs mimic the material qualities of the objects they are meant to evoke. Greek temples have decorative stone elements that look like the necessary features of wooden structures. The real wood siding on 1930s station wagons later morphs into the wood veneer on the family wagon in the 1960s. The phone icon on your cell is a handset of the kind you haven't used in decades. The skeuomorph is an affordance — a way to define how an object should or could be used. It's designed to create an instant familiarity and usability, a way to bypass the need for training in a new design language or order of operations. These kinds of affordances are not universally endorsed. Tech writer Clive Thompson maintains that skeuomorphs hobble innovation "by lashing designers to metaphors of the past," but the Interaction Design Foundation counters with an argument first applied to Lazarus, "skeuomorphism is dead, long live skeuomorphism."

Many entrepreneurs and development officials now look to California for guidance, wandering Silicon Valley trying to figure out start-up culture, high-tech spin-offs, and how to design a positive view of failure. Commercial real estate developers have long tried to figure out how L.A. developer Rick Caruso managed to combine Disney's place-making with a deep understanding the retail space when he created the Grove, an open-air mall that killed the development of enclosed malls across the entire United States. Even Minneapolis is building retail spaces as though there were no bomb cyclone winters in the Twin Cities. A skeuomorph buried in ice remains a skeuomorph in its wood-veneered heart.

An obeisance to free markets often blinded these visitors to the obvious: California had benefited for decades from massive public investment. Over a trillion inflation-adjusted dollars were pumped into the state by the federal government during the course of the 20th century. This money created lasting infrastructures for education, manufacturing, transportation, and communication, upon which later entrepreneurs depended.

California is only 160,000 square miles of the 57 million square miles of the Earth's surface, or a third of one percent of the habitable globe. To claim that the other 99.97 percent of the planet is but a skeuomorph of this state is economic, aesthetic, and social dominionism of the first order. But then again, isn't the simultaneous embrace and erasure of difference a defining characteristic of what neoliberalism is and does? The EU's ham-fisted austerity measures enacted after the recession of 2008 are Teutonic skeuomorphs of the original tax revolt, California's own Proposition 13, which showed politicians worldwide that you could design a new world order by appealing to middle-class stakeholders, encouraging them to uphold their privileges while leaving the wealthiest untouched, and making sure the next generation — often of people who didn't look like their older neighbors — stay stuck in place.

PROPOSITION 3: The California Design Dominion Is a Seductive *Gesamtkunstwerk*

The idea of California has always been utopic. It fuses the freedom of an open frontier (once cleared of its original inhabitants, of course), a gentle climate that allows for the cultivation of pretty much any delicacy (again, assuming an army of ultra-low-wage farm workers), and the growth of individuality, as distance lessened the controls otherwise exerted by families and churches. I've written elsewhere of the seductions of transcendental technologies that emerged in the Golden State during the 20th century from the New Age nostrums of Esalen to Scientology's baroque techno-catechism. But the design of the state and the state's designs gave birth to and were utterly consumed by a new idea: that the computer was not just "a" but "the" culture machine of the last quarter century, and that this culture machine itself embodies its Californian origins.

The seduction of technology is no more "natural" than its silicon components. Designers work hard at capturing attention and monetizing it. Back in the 1990s, Stanford's B. J. Fogg kluged together a new word, "captology" — from "computers as persuasive technologies" or CAPT. He set up a small lab to explore how users could be seduced into spending more time on whatever digital device they were using. Stanford students started to graduate from Fogg's lab just around the time that mobile telephones began morphing into mini-networked computers. Those devices, especially Apple's iPhone — distinguished, as always, by the fine and seductive phrase "Designed in California" — were quite literally tailor-made to execute Fogg's three-part plan for designing persuasive technologies: get specific, make it easy, and trigger the behavior. Dominion's *Gesamtkunstwerk* now had its marching orders.

PROPOSITION 4: The California Design Dominion Fuses Libertinism and Libertarianism into an Erotics of Individualized Consumption

Many of the chroniclers of the age — from Tracy Kidder to John Markoff to Brenda Laurel to Fred Turner — have noted how the NorCal libertine hippie ethos melded with SoCal's libertarian economics to imbue first the personal computer and then its more mobile descendants with a distinct market magic: purchasing them could bring liberation. The first generation of computer hackers still believed the idea that keeping things free and open would free and open the world. They were followed by generations of tinkerers, developers, and marketers who followed the dictum of their turtle-necked prophet Steve Jobs: "Real artists ship." He was redefining art as the production of deliverable commodities. To clarify, those who crave dominion can't just talk about markets, they have to flood them with salable product. It doesn't matter if that product is tangible, like computers or personal digital assistants, or immaterial, like websites and apps that are "free" only if the value of one's attention is literally zero.

Los Angeles's North Valley suburbs produce a torrent of pornography that streams globally 24/7 to every wired device not specifically blocked by government order or religious edict. Those electronic moans are certainly evidence that our solitude enhancement machines support an onanistic libertinism. But even those times when Silicon Valley chooses to follow an ascetic route, it emphasizes a market solipsism. The life- extending, ultra-low- calorie dieting, quantified self-exploring tech maven ascetics are still just consumers following their commodifiable bliss, just with a separate set of apps and products.

No matter, the single most important thing is to establish a revenue stream. The 21st-century grail of tech domination is to transcend nature itself, becoming that most seductive and yet impossible of creatures, the "unicorn." For the Silicon Valley venture capitalist, there is no greater object of lust than a privately held company valued over a billion dollars (inflation being an issue even for venture capitalists, there are now also "decacorns" valued over 10 billion).

PROPOSITION 5: The California Design Dominion Worships Oxymorons Like Billionaire Rebels and Sexy Geeks

The #MeToo moment began in California, linking stories of Google executives keeping sex slaves with the more tabloid-worthy reports of the Hollywood casting couch. And yet, both industries have always been explicit about their desires to dominate not only markets, but also whatever sexual partners came their way. "Unicorn" can refer both to a billion-dollar start-up and another rare find — a beautiful young woman interested in joining a tech bro and his partner for a threesome. This connection may not be a coincidence. There is an equation that combines desire and the freedom to profit: creating the new (or usually new-ish) imbues both the producer and the consumer with the true California spirit of rebelliousness. From Malibu to Marin, the rebel is lauded, not just as a figure on the edge, but also as someone ready, willing and able to save the world, to make it a better place, to share the love. As California Design Dominionists, these "revolutionaries" will be compensated at unicorn levels (with both money and sex) for inventing the future and keeping it entertained. Rather than maintaining firewalls between the economic and the erotic, the "disruptors" collapse all of life's distinctions into one continuous flow of consumption and production.

To do good and do well, to change the world like a Lenin or a Trotsky but to live like a Romanov or a Rockefeller, there's a dream that continues to animate.

PROPOSITION 6: The Design Genius of California Is Infectious

California has been the hotbed of designing and designating technologies to augment or fully replace the kinds of face-to-face human interactions that characterized the world before neoliberalism.

In San Francisco in 1967, Douglas Engelbart gave a public demonstration of his NLS, or oN-Line System, which laid out in working detail the way we live now.

The NLS offered collaborative, networked working environments in which hypertext, dynamic windows, graphical user interfaces, and video were all designed to function as a fluid, encompassing, connected, and ubiquitous whole. Whether it's the "mother of all demos," or the latest pitch by a Soylent-swigging techie to a room full of cynical venture capitalists, the point has been to augment the human psyche and sensorium via tools designed to improve workplace productivity and human happiness. Stanford's design program, otherwise known as d.school, evangelizes a gospel of "design thinking," thereby proselytizing to the rest of the world the California Design Dominion.

This "augmentation" of the human was a key goal of dominion. In 1967, the Oregon-born and -based poet and novelist Richard Brautigan was the poet-in-residence at the California Institute of Technology in Pasadena. At the culmination of his residency, he published 1,500 copies of a chapbook titled *All Watched Over by Machines of Loving Grace*, which he distributed for free, as he often did at that stage of his career. The title poem distills the essence of what augmentation might bring: a return to Edenic bliss.

> I like to think
> (it has to be!)
> of a cybernetic ecology
> where we are free of our labors
> and joined back to nature,
> returned to our mammal
> brothers and sisters,
> and all watched over
> by machines of loving grace.

This was the cybernetics of Marxian fantasy. Once Douglas Engelbart's machines developed enough grace, they were in his phrase, to "bootstrap" us past the wicked problems of poverty and disease, and into the very garden that Karl Marx invokes in *The German Ideology*, where communism,

> makes it possible for me to do one thing today and another tomorrow, to hunt in the morning, fish in the afternoon, rear cattle in the evening, criticize after dinner, just as I have a mind, without ever becoming hunter, fisherman, herdsman or critic.

PROPOSITION 7: The California Design Dominion Defines the Contemporary Creation and Distribution of Subjectivity

If the tech industry had emphasized "bootstrapping" rather than "liking" or "following," perhaps a different set of problems would have emerged as interconnectivity became ubiquitous. When Leonard Kleinrock sent the first internet message from his lab at UCLA to the Stanford Research Institute in Palo Alto in 1969, it did more than bridge the divide between south and north: that transmission reshaped human life. Rather than freeing us from work to live life, work has become life and life has become work. The boundaries between work and non-work elide and productivity is redefined as true happiness. This fits with designs that privilege measurable units.

As we design sensors into more and more of the physical world and create ways of breaking down ever more of our lived experiences into bits and bytes, the act of measuring becomes imperative. The California Design Dominion is both product and driver of metricization,

Sabrina Ratté, *BIOME IV* from Biomes series, 2017, video HD, courtesy of the artist.

which is in turn, key to the ontology of neoliberalism. If something can be measured, it should be measured; if it can be designed or retrofitted to be measured, it can be financialized; if it can be financialized, profits belong to those who designed the system in the first place.

In the realm of social media, more posts, likes, and followers means more connection, which means better integration of the individual to the user group, which equals happiness. In the globe's blue and white Facebook future, we will heart Eloi subjectivities that joyfully trade personal data for network access, or we will be Morlocks banging on skin drums with human bones.

PROPOSITION 8: Los Angeles's Requisite Narcissism Has Become Global

The headshot is the starting point for the nascent actor, it is the first opportunity to create the public "self." The young actor really does study these initial photographs — there's even a book for them, titled simply *8X10*, a selection of best "before-they-were-stars" headshots. The web offers headshots galore, of course, as it has come to offer all that we desire, but the best place to study them is *in situ* — not in casting offices or on the studio lot, but rather on the walls of Los Angeles's dry cleaners, restaurants, and shoe repair shops. This is where the analog headshot is destined to languish, where the headshots of a dead rock 'n' roll drummer shares wall space with the Penthouse Pet of February 1997 and the child star of a long-forgotten Fox family sitcom.

If the success of YouTubers and Instagram influencers has lessened the stranglehold of Hollywood over celebrity, this apparent decentralization is actually a sign of the global obsession with celebrity itself. The Children's Digital Media Center runs regular focus groups, and finds that young people aspire to fame more than anything else. Surveying 14-to-18-year-olds, a Kaiser Family Foundation study determined that almost a third of teens in the Washington, DC, metro area have gone beyond just *wanting* to be famous, to feeling that it is *likely* they will be famous. Is this because they can easily take and share pictures of themselves?

While front-facing camera phones debuted in 2003, it wasn't until 2010 that the designers of the iPhone 4 made a device that could be held at arm's length to record and broadcast oneself. The smart phone revolution combined with the self-documentation of social media transformed the headshot into the selfie. Duck-lipped pouts became a global standard of self-presentation, and the shallow Hollywood cliché globalized, changing the way people around the world interact with each other, one swipe, like, and retweet after another.

PROPOSITION 9: Neoliberal Economic Policies May Be Less Deadly to the Idea of Culture Than the Smart Phone

All over the world, neoliberal austerity cops scold the makers of culture and strive to strip them of any kind of support that isn't tied directly to the market. Why should the "public" be taxed for paintings, films, symphonies, poems, and dances that they a) don't understand, b) don't like, and c) can watch later on their laptops? The history of philistinism is long and offers at least a few counter-arguments, most too well known to repeat here. What's new, however, is the extent to which problems arise because the California Design Dominion eats culture and craps "content."

Content, unlike culture, is designed to be metricizable, likable, and portable from medium to medium. Under the California Design Dominion, the way people encounter culture has built-in safeguards — phones can transform any experience or object into content instantly. Read a book or watch a movie, the internet will transform any opinion you might have into the heady brew of fandom, or its complementary beverage, Haterade®™. The California Design Dominion ensures that there are at least two sides to every cultural event or object: whether the work feeds the narcissism of the obsessed consumer or that it falls into what I've come to term "fannui," describing any long-term fantasy investments that don't scratch a nostalgic itch or offer new pleasures.

As the great actor Omar Sharif once said, "When you watch a film you are in, you only watch yourself." Pity the work of art in the age of algorithmic likability.

PROPOSITION 10: The California Design Dominion Is Unimodern

The California Design Dominion cannot create more California, even as it overbuilds in the very areas most prone to fires, eroding coastlines, and earthquakes. But it does create a fully functioning virtual state in the global imagination.

In clearing out local culture and replacing it with metadata-driven content, the California-of-the-Mind trades in what I call "unimodernism." The global networked culture that originates in the Golden State is unimodern in the sense that modernism in all its variants becomes universal. This uniformity happens in their effect if not affect. In the California Design Dominion's unimodern era, as bits, online and in databases, a photo is a painting is an opera is a pop single.

PROPOSITION 11: Monetization in the Guise of Empowerment

One of the great business myths of the last quarter century is that Steve Jobs rolled into Southern California and disrupted the entertainment industry so powerfully that it never recovered. Like so many fables, though, it does point to real transformations: from the decimation of the music business to the transformation of movies into something you watch on your phone. But what if we look at the Apple-conquers-Hollywood myth as a story about hybrid creatures — a mutual exchange of DNA, all taking place within the ecosystem we call California. If Hollywood is digitized, is Silicon Valley in turn Disneyfied?

Disneyfication, it should be noted, is not merely about smoothing the rough edges of life, it is about absorbing other cultures and homogenizing and monetizing them. Disney himself did this with the world's fairy tales. He understood that those stories were written in a different era, for children who were surrounded by death. Twentieth-century children, however, were protected by vaccines and penicillin — they needed inspiration more than warnings. The Little Mermaid dies at the end of the Hans Christian Andersen's 1837 tale, but of course, in the 1989 Disney animated version, she defeats the evil sea witch, marries the prince, and lives

Fountain, Installation view at Visitor Welcome Center

Alexandre Dorriz, *Occident, galloping / Gilgamesh, swimming ; ML/OL 01-09 [Zoopraxiscope A (1/3)]*, (6) Xerox on Aluminum, Pomegranate (35°39'10.151" N 119°53'35.837), Conduit holder, Retail hanger, Binder Clip, Stainless Steel Cord. 2019. Courtesy of artist and Visitor Welcome Center.

Alexandre Dorriz, *Untitled Mirage 02-02 [First Study for Shah Qajar Chador 01: Occident and L'Orient (Zoopraxiscope B)], or an Exhibitionary Complex (The Lynda and Stewart Resnick Cultural Center No. 3)*, Cyanotype on Cotton Canvas (Inner Ring Exposure Time & Location 18:44/03.10.19;35.6539;-119.8927/CA-33 ; Outer Ring Exposure Time & Location 11:19/03.12.19;34.0638;-118.3595/), Pistachios (Iran), Exposed Silk (3 Silkworm Cocoons exposed to VHS tape of "Lawrence of Arabia : Tape 1" played continually for appx. 100 days), Cotton and Linen Rope, Pipe, Bolts. 2019. Courtesy of artist and Visitor Welcome Center.

Alexandre Dorriz, *Untitled Mirage 09 (Fountain)*, Eye Wash Station, Galvanized Steel Pipes, Donation Box, Pond Pump, Potable Water (Caltech Resnick Institute : 4,820 mL ; Los Angeles County Museum of Art, Resnick Pavilion : 4,789 mL ; Hammer Museum : 4,139 mL ; Resnick Center for Food Law and Policy at UCLA School of Law : 4,039 mL). 2018 work in situ, completed 2019. Courtesy of artist and Visitor Welcome Center.

happily ever after. This process turns folk culture into an endlessly monetizable series of media products, from Halloween costumes to video games to The Wonderful World of Disney Presents the Little Mermaid Live!, a musical television special. But what of the 20th century's so-called "popular" or "mass" cultures?

Go out on Halloween, or during any other "carnivalesque" festivities around the globe. Observe the endless parade of little girls in Disney princess gowns and the little boys in Captain Jack Sparrow gear from *Pirates of the Caribbean*. The latter demonstrates the movement of content from medium to medium: a ride at Disneyland — first opened in 1967 and the last to be personally overseen by Disney himself before his death — becomes a live action film franchise in 2003. Disney's influence now extends far beyond the companies own animations, movies, and theme parks. Disney has also acquired many other brands and intellectual properties. Think about all the kids and grownups dressed as Pixar characters, from Buzz Lightyear the astronaut to Nemo the fish. There's also plenty of revelers dressed as our new gods: Marvel superheroes in padded chest plates and plastic masks; Jedi Knights swinging battery-powered lightsabers, wearing ill-fitting robes.

The colonization of our popular culture and imagination by a single company is not exceptional to Halloween or Disney. For many around the globe, Facebook is a way to access the rest of the internet via a blue-and white interface (founder Mark Zuckerberg is color blind, and chose his design schemata accordingly).

While deactivating Facebook is made difficult by design, so is avoiding its subsidiaries. Preferring Instagram (which Zuckerberg acquired 2012) to Facebook, or WhatsApp (2014) to Messenger is akin to dressing as Pixar's Mr. Incredible (which Disney acquired in 2006), Marvel's Hulk (2009), or Lucasfilm's ultimate villain, Darth Vader (2012). Wherever you choose to direct your attention, your cash, or your cosplay, you feed the same central controlling corporations somewhere in California.

PROPOSITION 12: The California Design Dominion Traffics in Totalization

Under the California Design Domain, the attention paid to virtual experiences like Facebook or a Google search, or the funds spent on branded goods are essentially the same. No matter how many services, experiences, and objects are sold with the promise of liberating consumers — freeing them from toil, from boredom, and limits to communication — the very design of these services, experiences and objects locks their users into programs that monetize the flow of data. The California Design Dominion brands and incentivizes consumption at every turn and creates services that loop users into ever more encompassing and inescapable networks.

In a neat bit of reverse corporate procreation, Google spun off Alphabet as its own parent company in 2015. Google's motto had famously been "Don't Be Evil," but Alphabet chose something different: "Do the Right Thing." Alphabet's motto allows for moral flexibility — it raises the question "Right for whom?"

The California Design Dominion has algorithms, scripts, metrics, and surveys to determine what's "right" for stakeholders (that's not you, by the way, unless you own their stock), and can measure that rectitude in user bases, downloads, and revenue flows. Tweaking these metrics fruitfully creates systems and habits that bind ever-larger global populations into California-ness, not a state so much as a totalized state of being and mind.

PROPOSITION 13: The Greatest Dream That California Sells Is the Idea That in Its Sun-Kissed Embrace You Can Do What You Love

This is the promise and the premise of California Design Dominion.

¤

SELECTED BIBLIOGRAPHY

Andy Cameron and Richard Barbrook, "The California Ideology," *MUTE* v. 1, n. 3 (1995).

Antonio Gramsci, *The Prison Notebooks* (CRC Press and Macat Library, 2017[orig. 1948]).

Jacques Derrida, "The Other's Language: Jacques Derrida Interviews Ornette Coleman, 23 June 1997," trans. Timothy S. Murphy, *Genre* 1 (June, 2004).

Jean Baudrillard, *America* (Verso, 1989).

Christa Wolf, *City of Angels or, The Overcoat of Dr Freud* (Farrar, Straus and Giroux, 2013).

Peter Lunenfeld, "State of Transcendence: Spiritual Technologies and the California Dream," in Justin McGuirk and Brendan McGetrick, eds. *California: Designing Freedom* (London: Phaidon/Design Museum, 2017) and *The Secret War Between Downloading and Uploading: How the Computer Became Our Culture Machine* (Cambridge, MA: MIT Press, 2011).

B.J. Fogg, *Persuasive Technology: Using Computers to Change What We Think and Do* (Morgan Kaufmann Publishers, 2002).

Tracy Kidder, *The Soul of a New Machine* (Little Brown, 1981).

John Markoff, *What the Dormouse Said: How the 60s Counterculture Shaped the Personal Computer Industry* (Penguin, 2005).

Fred Turner, *From Counterculture to Cyberculture: Stewart Brand, the Whole Earth Network and the Rise of Digital Utopianism* (University of Chicago Press, 2006).

Brenda Laurel, *Utopian Entrepreneur*, design Denise Gonzales-Crisp (MIT Press, 2001).

Thierry Bardini, *Bootstrapping: Douglas Engelbart, Coevolution, and the Origins of Personal Computing* (Stanford University Press, 2000).

Thanks to Arden Stern and Sami Siegelbaum for inviting me to give an early version of these propositions at their 2018 College Art Association panel, "Design and Neo-Liberalism."

CONTRIBUTORS

J.D. Daniels is the winner of a 2016 Whiting Award and *The Paris Review*'s 2013 Terry Southern Prize. *The Correspondence* (Farrar, Straus and Giroux) was published in 2017. His writing has appeared in *Esquire, The Paris Review, n+1, Oxford American, The Los Angeles Review of Books* and elsewhere, including *The Best American Essays* and *The Best American Travel Writing.*

Carolina De Robertis is a writer of Uruguayan origin. She is the author of four novels, most recently *Cantoras,* a finalist for the Kirkus Prize and a New York Times Editors' Choice. Her books have been translated into seventeen languages and have received a Stonewall Book Award, Italy's Rhegium Julii Prize, and a fellowship from the National Endowment for the Arts, among other honors. She is also an award-winning translator of Latin American and Spanish literature, and editor of the anthology *Radical Hope: Letters of Love and Dissent in Dangerous Times.* She teaches at San Francisco State University, and lives in Oakland, California, with her wife and two children.

Michelle Dominique Burke is a poet and a PhD Fellow in the University of Houston's Literature and Creative Writing Department. She lives in Houston.

Maud Doyle holds a Master of Fine Arts from Columbia and a Master of Theological Studies from Harvard. She is a writer based in New York City.

Camille Dungy is a poet, essayist and editor whose eight books include *Trophic Cascade, Guidebook to Relative Strangers: Journeys into Race, Motherhood and History*, and *Black Nature: Four Centuries of African American Nature Poetry*. A 2019 Guggenheim Fellow, her other honors include NEA Fellowships in poetry and prose, an American Book Award, and two NAACP Image Award nominations. Dungy is a professor at Colorado State University.

A.H. Jerriod Avant is a native of Longtown, Mississippi. He's received scholarships from the Breadloaf Writer's Conference and Naropa University's Summer Writing Program. His poems have appeared in *Mississippi Review, Callaloo, Ecotone, Boston Review, Virginia Quarterly Review*, and other journals. A recipient of two Winter Fellowships from the Fine Arts Work Center in Provincetown, Jerriod is currently a PhD English student and teaching assistant at the University of Rhode Island. He lives and teaches in Kingston, Rhode Island.

Edgar Kunz is the author of *Tap Out* (Mariner/HMH, 2019), a *New York Times* New & Noteworthy book. His work has been supported by fellowships and awards from the Academy of American Poets, the National Endowment for the Arts, the MacDowell Colony, and Stanford University, where he was a Wallace Stegner Fellow. He lives in Baltimore, Maryland, where he teaches at Goucher College and in the Newport MFA.

Amy Leach is the author of *Things That Are* (Milkweed, 2012) and Beasts in the Margins, forthcoming from Farrar, Straus & Giroux. Her work has appeared in *Best American Essays*, and she has been recognized with a Whiting Award and a Rona Jaffe Foundation Writers' Award. She lives in Montana.

Timothy Liu is the author of ten books of poems, including *Of Thee I Sing*; *Say Goodnight*; and *Vox Angelica*, which won the 1992 Poetry Society of America's Norma Farber First Book Award. He has also edited *Word of Mouth: An Anthology of Gay American Poetry*. Liu's poems have appeared in such places as *Best American Poetry, Bomb, Kenyon Review, The Nation, Paris Review, Ploughshares, Poetry, The Pushcart Prize, Virginia Quarterly Review* and *The Yale Review*. His journals and papers are archived in the Berg Collection at the New York Public Library. He is currently a Professor of English at William Paterson University in New Jersey.

Peter Lunenfeld works at the intersection of media studies, art criticism, design theory, digital humanities, and urban history. In 2020, Viking will publish *City at the Edge of Forever: Stories from an Infinite Los Angeles*. He is the vice chair of UCLA's Design Media Arts department.

Claire McEachern teaches literature of the English Renaissance at the University of California, Los Angeles, and farms with her family in Malibu, CA.

Geoff Nicholson is a contributing editor to the *Los Angeles Review of Books*. His books include the novels *Bleeding London* and *The Hollywood Dodo*. His latest novel is *The Miranda*.

Jason Porter is the author of the novel *Why Are You So Sad?* and host of the short fiction podcast Grownups Are Lucky. He is currently at work on a collection of 250 stories all 250 words in length.

Molly Prentiss is the author of the novel *Tuesday Nights in 1980*. She lives in Brooklyn.

Ellie Robins is a writer and translator whose work has appeared in the *Guardian*, the *Washington Post*, the *TLS*, the *LA Times*, the *LA Review of Books*, and elsewhere. A Londoner by birth, she now lives in Los Angeles and has worked as an editor in Buenos Aires and New York. Her writing circles place, narrative, and the climate crisis.

Roger S. Gottlieb is professor of philosophy at Worcester Polytechnic Institute and the author or editor of 21 books on political philosophy, ethics, religious studies, contemporary spirituality, and the environmental crisis. Recipient of two Nautilus Book Awards (for *Spirituality: What it Is and Why it Matters* and *Engaging Voices: Tales of Morality and Meaning in an Age of Global Warming*), his most recent book is *Morality and the Environmental Crisis* (Cambridge University Press).

Aisha Sabatini Sloan is the author of the essay collections, *The Fluency of Light* and *Dreaming of Ramadi in Detroit*. She is the Helen Zell Visiting Professor of Creative Nonfiction at the University of Michigan.

Janet Sarbanes is the author of the short fiction collections *Army of One* (Otis Press/Seismicity Editions) and *The Protester Has Been Released* (C & R Press). The recipient of a 2017 Creative Capital/Andy Warhol art writer's grant, Sarbanes has also published art criticism and other critical writing in museum catalogues, anthologies, and journals. Her essay on Shaker aesthetics and utopian communalism received the Eugenio Battisti prize from the Society for Utopian Studies. Sarbanes teaches in the MFA Creative Writing Program at CalArts.

Malcolm Tariq is poet and playwright from Savannah, Georgia. He is the author of *Heed the Hollow* (Graywolf Press, 2019), winner of the 2018 Cave Canem Poetry Prize, and *Extended Play* (Gertrude Press, 2017). A graduate of Emory University, Malcolm has a PhD in English from the University of Michigan. He lives in New York City.

Matthew Zapruder is the author of five collections of poetry, most recently *Father's Day*, from Copper Canyon in Fall 2019, as well as *Why Poetry*, a book of prose. He is editor at large at Wave Books, and teaches in the MFA and English Department at Saint Mary's College of California.

FEATURED ARTISTS

John Baldessari (b. 1931; National City, CA) is a pioneering Santa Monica, CA-based conceptual artist whose experimentation across a range of media (collage, printmaking, video/film, photography, digital art, painting, and performance) developed into a defining aesthetic that appropriates mass culture and plays with established conventions and physical form to decontextualize, juxtapose, repeat, and create language, text, and found imagery or objects, particularly in relation to the media, art, and film industries. He is a key founder of Southern California Conceptualism, an influential educator of younger artists, and a legend of postmodern art in the late 20th Century.

Lauren Bon is an environmental artist from Los Angeles, CA. Her practice, Metabolic Studio, explores self-sustaining and self-diversifying systems of exchange that feed emergent properties that regenerate the life web. Some of her works include: *Not A Cornfield*, which transformed and revived an industrial brownfield in downtown Los Angeles into a thirty-two-acre cornfield for one agricultural cycle; *100 Mules Walking the Los Angeles Aqueduct*, a 240-mile performative action that aimed to reconnect the city of Los Angeles with the source of its water for the centenary of the opening of the Los Angeles Aqueduct. Her studio's current work, *Bending the River Back into the City*, aims to utilize Los Angeles' first private water right to deliver 106-acre feet of water annually from the LA River to over 50 acres of land in the historic core of downtown LA. This model can be replicated to regenerate the 52-mile LA River, reconnect it to its floodplain and form a citizens' utility.

The Center for Land Use Interpretation (CLUI) is a research and education organization dedicated to the increase and diffusion of knowledge about how the nation's lands are apportioned, utilized, and perceived. The Center is interested in understanding the nature and extent of human interaction with the surface of the earth, and in finding new meanings in the intentional and incidental forms that we individually and collectively create. Founded in 1994, it has produced dozens of exhibits on land use themes and regions for the CLUI's own exhibit spaces, as well as for public institutions all over the United States, and overseas. The Center publishes books, conducts public tours, and offers information and research resources that examine, describe, and explain the built landscape in America.

Alexandre Dorriz (b. Los Angeles, CA) is a research-based artist informed by fieldwork and archiving practices investigating auto-Orientalism, memory, optics, and fiber. In an ongoing series (2014-), he has archived his maternal family's history of working with and collecting textiles for four generations, much of the collection smuggled into North America during the Iranian Diaspora of the 1970s and repurposed as gowns by his mother in the 1990s. His current research is in finding memory seriations in silk fiber protein, breeding silkworms to investigate how temporal indices appear in silk cocoons and modeling localized economies in an intermittent studio installation entitled, "Economies of Small, or the Location of Capital". His practice studies formal interpretations of interchangeable lens and optical-based systems to examine representation and memory, including representations of geographies through refraction and the sampling of water. Dorriz received his MFA at the University of Southern California and his BA at the University of California, Berkeley.

LAND (Los Angeles Nomadic Division) is a non-profit organization founded in 2009 committed to curating site-specific public art exhibitions in Los Angeles and beyond. LAND believes that all people deserve the opportunity to experience innovative contemporary art in their everyday existence, to enhance their quality of life and ways of thinking about their community. In turn, artists deserve the opportunity to realize projects in the public realm, unsupported through traditional institutions. LAND brings contemporary art outside of the walls of museums and galleries, into our shared public spaces and unique sites, in Los Angeles and beyond.

Hanieh Khatibi's work explores notions of precariousness and uncertainty in conditional beings or self-made situations. Alongside a concern with gender and the body as a site of suffering, birth, death, and joy, she seeks to investigate the ongoing, ever-changing relationship of mankind to that which we call nature. Strategies of placement and displacement, formation and transformation are designed to interrogate and reconfigure the body itself. By adopting the language of performativity and reactivating the self, Khatibi is chasing the very overlap between restriction and possibility, which is to say that she is attempting to traverse and map a particularly liminal space. By staging in different places and varying durations or imposing resistance and limitation upon the body, it becomes a sculptural object that must react and adapt. Observation, personal events and historical documents lead the formation of this practice. Khatibi works across a variety of media including performance installation, video, photography, object making and drawing. Khatibi was born and raised in Tehran, Iran and recently received an MFA from the California Institute of the Arts. She currently lives and works in Los Angeles.

Satoshi Kojima (b. 1979, Tokyo, Japan) is a painter currently based in Dusseldorf, Germany. Kojima attended Tokyo Zokei University and received his Master of Arts at Kunstakademie Dusseldorf, Germany in 2014. His solo exhibitions include, *Chaste As Ice Pure As Snow*, TRAMPS, New York, NY (2019); *Delicate Boss*, TRAMPS, London, United Kingdom (2017); *Satoshi Kojima*, Bridget Donahue, New York, NY (1017); *Satoshi Kojima*, TRAMPS London, United Kingdom (2014) and *Ohne Titel*, Grau6, Dusseldorf, Germany (2010). Recent group exhibitions include *Eggy and Seedy*, organized by Matt Copson and Alastair MacKinven, Reading International, Reading, United Kingdom (2017); *CFA Classics*, Contemporary Fine Arts - CFA Berlin, Berlin, Germany (2015); *Smilies*, Parkhaus im Malkastenpark, Dusseldorf, Germany (2015); *Marie Karlberg /* Satoshi Kojima, TRAMPS at Nansengade 62, Copenhagen, Denmark (2015); *Lady Work Work*, TRAMPS London, United Kingdom (2014) and *Klasse Doig*, Display Gallery, London, United Kingdom (2014) among others.

Latefa Noorzai, born 1960 in Kabul, Afghanistan, is an artist currently practicing at Creative Growth, a nonprofit that serves artists with disabilities in Oakland, California. Noorzai, a native Farsi speaker and immigrant to the United States, quickly established her studio practice at Creative Growth despite obstacles of communication and cultural navigation. Noorzai's tenacity is demonstrated in her bold portrait paintings inspired by a plethora of source material. Latefa's strong and stark outlines provide loose structure for the heavy and confident brush strokes that fill her figures with dynamic expression and presence. Noorzai's work has been featured at Outsider Art Fair in Paris and New York, D'Dessin Art Fair in Paris, Good Luck Gallery in Los Angeles, and is included in Hannah Rieger›s permanent Art Brut Collection.

Sabrina Ratté is a Canadian artist whose practice includes video, animation, installations, sculptures, audio-visual performances and prints. Mixing analog technologies, photography and 3D animation techniques, her work focuses on the creation of architectures, abstract compositions and surreal landscapes. In 2019 she was longlisted for the Sobey Art Award (CAN). Previous exhibitions: Laforet Museum (Japan), Musée National des Beaux-arts du Québec, Thoma Foundation (Santa Fe), Dolby (San Francisco), Young Project Gallery (Los Angeles), Whitney Museum of Art (New York), Galerie Charlot (Paris), Chronus Art Center, (Shanghai), Künstlerhaus Bethanien (Berlin), HEK (Basel), Museum of the Moving Image (New York), Ellephant Gallery (Montreal).

LeRoy Stevens (born 1984) lives and works in Los Angeles. Recent exhibitions include *Small World Somewhere Street*, The Box, Los Angeles (2019), *FMS BWTÖZÄU PGGIV-..?MÜ (FOR STEPHEN FOSTER)*, Shane Campbell Gallery, Chicago (2019), *Floating World*, Potts, Los Angeles (2018), Books, Chan Gallery, Pomona College, Claremont (2016), *Oskar*, The Finley, Los Angeles (2015), *Tilde*, Nathalie Karg, New York (2014), *Starting Blocks*, Jancar Gallery, Los Angeles (2014) and *From the Bird's Mouth*, Linnagalerii, Tallinn (2011). Since 2009, Stevens has published artist's records through his label Small World. His work has been written about in the *NY Times*, *The Daily Telegraph* and he has appeared on NPR, BBC and KCHUNG.

Oscar Tuazon (b. 1975, Seattle) lives and works in Los Angeles. The artist was most recently the subject of solo shows at Bellevue Arts Museum, *Oscar Tuazon: Collaborator* and at the Aspen Art Museum, *Oscar Tuazon: Fire Worship*. Other recent solo shows include *Oscar Tuazon: Water School* at MSU Broad Museum; a large-scale installation Une colonne d'eau in the Place Vendôme, Paris in 2017, *Oscar Tuazon: Hammer Projects*, at the Hammer Museum, Los Angeles in 2016 and Studio, at Le Consortium, Dijon, France in 2015. *Los Angeles Water School (LAWS)* is a functional artwork, an experimental school for students of all ages to engage in dialogue and collaborative work with water. Located adjacent to the Los Angeles River, in a structure inspired by Steve and Holly Baer's self-sufficient passive solar *Zome House* (1969-72), LAWS is the first of four Water Schools planned by artist Oscar Tuazon, with locations in Minnesota, Michigan, and Nevada. Presented by LAND, this series of events builds a genealogy of the complex life of water in Los Angeles, through the lens of local history, architecture, politics, and art.

Mario Ybarra Jr. (b. 1973, Los Angeles, CA; lives and works in Wilmington, CA) is a visual and performance artist, educator, founding member of Slanguage collective, and activist who combines street culture with fine art to produce site-specific urban interventions that often bring to light little-known aspects of a particular location's cultural history. Ybarra Jr.'s chapter of *The Manifest Destiny Billboard Project* used source material from the artist's ongoing collection of images of what he calls "barrio aesthetics" in Los Angeles, transplanting these images to billboards spread throughout Mobile, AL. Ybarra Jr. is interested in inserting the daily culture and experience of one city and neighborhood into another, creating artworks that are both contrasting and familiar.